IN HIS CHRYSALIS

Transformed by God through My Dad's 32-year Coma

WRITTEN BY

JUDY PEREZ VELAZQUEZ

DEDICATION

My Heroes Wear My Genes

In Dedication

To my dad, who audibly heard the voice of the Lord say, "Times have changed, but I AM still the same," and then, without saying a word, introduced us all to *the great I AM*.

In Gratitude

To my mom, the wind beneath my wings, whose "yes" to Jesus, my dad, and me literally changed the trajectory of countless lives forever, especially mine. I am who I am because you loved us fiercely and valiantly fought to ensure our home was anchored to Jesus. Your story is so much more incredible and exemplary than mine - thank you for living it faithfully and being the blueprint for me to journey in my own life. Sending you *butterfly kisses* throughout the pages of this book.

Enamored

With my beloved José. When God looked to bring me someone far beyond *my list* of dreams, He knew no one else could surpass you. My story in print is because you championed me to write it, all the while living it right alongside me since we were teenagers. You've always believed in me, seen me beyond all my flaws, and loved me unconditionally. You continually make all my dreams come true. There's absolutely no one else I love like you.

Entrusted

To my four treasures: Caitlyn, Karissa, Joscelyn, and Joseph. Know that I look at each of you individually and I'm truly in awe that God would give me the privilege and honor to be your mommy. Remember there is a legacy of love, strength, and determination deep within your bones of people who have gone before you to trailblaze, make the road straight, and lay the foundation for your lives. Despite our shortcomings, we've ensured your roots run deep so you can reach higher than any one of us ever will. Each of you have your *own* amazing story to live and tell. I love watching it unfold.

Indebted
To Jesus, the center of it all.

Inspire my writing as you inspired the authors of your Word.

CONTENTS

*Now to Him who is able to do far more abundantly than all that we ask or think, **according to the power at work within us**, to Him be glory in the church and in Christ Jesus throughout all generations, forever and ever. Amen."* – Ephesians 3:20-21, emphasis mine

EMBRYO STAGE – *Eggs are the first stage of the Butterfly Life Cycle. Each embryo is filled with nutritious fluid that the developing caterpillar uses for its grow*

LARVA STAGE – *The caterpillar is like an eating machine, only resting to digest its food*

FOREWORD

In my career as an author for over twenty-two years, I have met some extraordinary people in both my travels and in my writing ministry; but never have I met anybody quite as unique as Judy. Judy's experiences and the things she's survived have molded her into an expert at navigating through hardships and the unexpected terms life brings.

Not only is she able to face these trials head on, but she excels at it with the beautiful grace of God. She sets the example for everyone in that, while she has her own suffering, she never fails to care for others. She is an extraordinary woman – not because she's perfect, but because she has turned her imperfections, her mistakes, and her own personal journey into tutors to grow into the amazing woman she is today.

Judy is an inspiration to women all over the world and it is an honor to write the foreword of her first book. Anybody who reads this book will not only be blessed, but transformed in the way they see God and the way they see life.

– Sheri Rose Shepherd,
Author of Eight Best-Selling Books
His Princess Ministries

INTO HIS CHRYSALIS

I emerge from the chrysalis once again
Throughout the whole process, God has been my friend
Gone away the uncertainty and fear
Forever in His grasp, He was always near

"Shape me and mold me," at first I had said
So into the chrysalis, I was lovingly led
Wrapped gently, yet firmly, in His mighty embrace
To be transformed into a reflection of His face

Some seasons I lived in silence and others in dark solitude
Moments of misunderstanding and stages of gratitude
There were moments when it hurt and I writhed in pain
Yet always encouraged by the One who was slain

To go into the chrysalis designed just for me
Is to know that I will emerge as He fashioned me to be
Another piece refined, another rough edge made smooth
Closer to His plan for my life I can confidently move

I fear to go back in for what it might cost
I fear more not finding my place in His will for the lost
So back into the chrysalis I obediently go
Jesus, yes He loves me, truly this one thing I know!

INTRODUCTION

There are roughly twenty thousand species of butterflies in the world. Each one is unique. Each has its own process, its own journey. Just like us. We are all different with our own path only we can take.

Unlike us, however, butterflies go through a morphological process only once and then die. They begin as a tiny embryo, eat their way out as a caterpillar, then enter the pupa stage as a chrysalis. Finally, they emerge as a majestic *imago*, or the adult butterflies that grace the skies before us. Everything about their lives is limited – what they are, what they do, and where they go. Their existence is *finite*.

But for *us*, the process of transformation is limitless! In the very beginning of our relationship with Him, God's love for us draws us to Him as our Savior, Helper, and Friend. Our very being longs for something, *someone,* more than what we can do for ourselves. Some of us immediately recognize that only God satisfies the soul. For others, it is a journey through many wrong venues, which brings us to the mercy seat of God where we come to realize *solo Dios*, only God can be the true love we've been looking for. There's a reason why asking Jesus into your heart and getting saved is called being "born again." Like the metamorphosis of a caterpillar into a butterfly, believers experience a life-altering, beautiful transformation.

When we first acquire that "first love," all we do is hunger for God, His Word, and His will for our lives. We are like that little caterpillar growing and eating, learning everything we can! We feed on pages and pages of Scripture where we can "taste and see that the Lord is good" (Psalm 34:8). Every day is a new adventure, a new insight, a new opportunity in our new life with the Lord. We want anyone and everyone to know what God is doing so they can experience the same things we are enjoying.

But along the way, something changes.

Not everything is as "wonderful" as it once seemed. Not everyone wants to join in the celebration. Some people misunderstand us. We may feel restrained from accomplishing all the things we want to do for God. There are moments of darkness and times of problems, worries, and fears. Moments of confusion and even regret that we've been placed into a situation where we can't even imagine what the purpose could be for entering that "chrysalis." We may even stop hearing God. He can seem silent, so far away . . .

But if we hold on tight to His promises in Scripture . . .

If we prevail in our prayer times whether we hear His answer or not . . .

If we wait patiently on the Lord, knowing He hears our cry . . .

If we remember, above any other truth in the world, that God *loves* us . . .

We will emerge, realizing all the while we were being refined and defined into more of His likeness, His *imago*!

2 Corinthians 3:18 says, "So all of us who have had that veil removed can see and reflect the glory of the Lord. And the Lord – who is the Spirit – **makes us more and more like Him** as we are changed into His glorious image" *(NLT, emphasis mine)*. The amazing thing is, it doesn't end there.

We never "arrive" at the end, but we go through the whole process again and again . . . which can make us shudder with trepidation *and* excitement at the same time.

So, this is my story. These are glimpses of my journey into multiple seasons I found myself in God's chrysalis, emerging transformed each time, very much aware that God has been with me through it all.

While, I admit, most days I still only see myself as a green, squishy, crawling thing, God has been so merciful with me – especially in the chrysalis stages of life. He has allowed me to *emerge* as a more beautiful creation, *flutter* my wings, and *soar*.

I love Him so!

I encourage you to see God for all of who He is. My hope as we journey together is that you, too, will see that, regardless of what life brings your way, there is absolutely, unequivocally no better place to be than . . .

IN HIS CHRYSALIS!

EMBRYO STAGE

Eggs are the first stage of a butterfly's life cycle. Each egg is filled with nutritious fluid that the developing caterpillar uses for its growth. Some caterpillars wait till Spring to hatch, while others hatch in just two weeks. The egg is usually laid under a leaf so birds and other prey don't find it. It is glued on hard to prevent predators from walking off with it.

"Being fragile doesn't mean you're weak. All your life you fight for one goal and you make it happen no matter how far the journey is. True strength lies on the inside, not the outside."

~ Joscelyn Analei

Chapter One

I KNOW THE PLANS I HAVE FOR YOU

"For I know the plans I have for you," declares the Lord. "Plans for welfare and not for evil, to give you a future and a hope. Then you will call upon me and come and pray to me, and I will hear you. You will seek me and find me, when you seek me with all your heart."
Jeremiah 29:11-13

One of the last things Dad ever did was pretend to raise me up in the air, smile as if he were looking at me, and say, "Judy, Judy." I was three months old.

Until then, my dad had been the church's youth leader at Templo El Buen Pastor in Fullerton, California. Not long before he got sick, my dad told my mom he had heard the voice of the Lord. It wasn't just in his heart; a clear and *audible* voice had told him, "Peter, times have changed, but *I AM* still the same."

Dad knew the Lord was calling him to a *new* ministry. He told Mom he would resign as youth leader and prepare to do whatever the Lord asked of him. Dad got all their important documents in order and waited to hear what the Lord would guide him to do next.

I was born on March 30, 1975. Not long afterward, Dad came home with a terrible headache and fever. What doctors initially thought was a severe case of the flu turned into a 106°F fever with hallucinations. He was rushed to the emergency room. Dad had been infected by spinal meningitis and encephalitis, complicated by tuberculosis. Back in 1975, it wasn't as easily recognizable as it is now.

Doctors drained the accumulating liquid from my dad's rapidly swelling brain by drilling a hole in his head and placing a shunt. He had stopped breathing, which led to an emergency tracheotomy.

Each month went by with one complication after another. Before Mom knew it, a year had passed and my twenty-five-year-old dad had suffered so much brain damage that he was a quadriplegic, could no longer move his arms or legs, was blind, and would never speak again. He was on life support, fed by a G-tube in his stomach, and said to be in a vegetative state.

By the time my mom turned twenty-four, she had spent an entire year by Dad's side, coming home only to feed me and rest before going back again. Throughout her time at the hospital, she signed a myriad of forms and agreed to so many different procedures, she'd lost count. Finally, Mom faced one last decision: whether or not to take Dad off of life support.

The doctor urged her that it was time to "let him go." If he lived, it was suggested Mom put Dad in a nursing home and "get on" with her life. After all, she was still young, attractive enough to easily start her life over, and she had to think of her little girl, who would never really know her daddy, anyway.

Mom carried so much responsibility in the decision she had to make. Although no one saw Him, Mom knew she had never been alone in that hospital; the Lord had her and Dad in the palm of His hand, keeping them safe, giving Mom wisdom with every decision, and sustaining Dad's life. Mom went to the Lord for guidance. Dad was her best friend, the only man she had ever known, the father of her child, and the love of her life.

When my mom, Rita Lopez, was a teenager, she was giddy when the choir from the nearby Bible college full of handsome, single young men sang at her church. She looked up and saw *him*. He was indeed tall, dark, and handsome. With an illusion of teenage fantasy, Mom pointed to him and whispered to her friend, "I'm going to marry *that* one."

Two years later, she found herself at that very same Bible college: Latin American Bible Institute (LABI College) in La Puente, California, which dedicated itself to training men and women to serve as pastors, missionaries, evangelists, and lay ministers. Mom made many lifelong friends at LABI College. One in particular was a tall Puerto Rican named Peter Perez. He played the bass for the school choir and was in a group called "The Royal Singers." Mom, who had been playing piano since she was thirteen, played at church and easily became the pianist for their choir at school as well. They began dating. Only later did the Lord open Mom's eyes to the memory of when she was a teenager and had claimed Dad in her heart a couple of years before.

Dad graduated in May of 1972, and Mom graduated in May of 1973. The next month, my parents were married. She never could've imagined only three years later she'd have to decide whether or not to take her husband off life support.

Mom told the Lord that if He chose to take my dad home to Heaven, she would submit to His will. But, if the Lord saw it fit to let Dad live, she promised the Lord – just as she had promised her husband – she would take care of him *herself* for the rest of their lives.

When the doctors removed all the machines that were "sustaining" his life, Dad started breathing on his own. God alone sustained my daddy's life and would do so for many, many years to follow.

On her own, and with the guidance of Holy Spirit, Mom learned how to care for Dad. Her days consisted of bathing him, changing the dressings from his tracheotomy procedure and his gastrostomy tube site, feeding Dad through his G-tube, and giving him medications. Mom learned to read Dad so well in the thirty-two years she cared for him at home, she could predict an oncoming seizure, what illness he was coming down with, if he was hungry or needed to be repositioned in his bed, and whether he had a headache. Anything and everything that had to do with my dad, she knew exactly what it was.

Wanting to keep life as "normal" for our family as possible, we celebrated Dad's birthdays with my cousins every year. Mom made sure Dad always had the latest hairstyles. We decorated his room to match the seasons. We never knew how much he understood about the world around him or that the years were passing by.

Mom would reach out and gently take Dad's hand to put it in mine as if he was holding my hand.

"See, Peter, this is your daughter Judy's hand. Can you feel her hand?"

But it was her, not him, who was reaching out to hold me. He couldn't fold his fingers to hold mine. As I looked down at his hand over mine, my *heart* tried to pretend he truly was holding my hand the way all the other daddies did as they walked with their children. But my *mind* knew it just wasn't the same.

On rare and precious occasions throughout the years, Mom would yell excitedly for me to come to Dad's room quickly. Standing beside him she would ask, "Peter, if you love us, close your eyes tight." And he *would!*

On those days, Dad somehow seemed more "conscious" than others. Perhaps small synapses in his brain triggered at just the right moment and, all of a sudden, Mom would just know that Dad was "awake." She sensed Dad was keenly aware of what was going on and he could only respond by shaking his head, closing his eyes, or puckering his lips to give Mom a kiss. We'd hear her yell and everyone in the house would rush in.

In those few minutes the Lord granted us *real* time with Dad, we tried to catch him up to date on how well we were doing so he knew we were okay. We would update him as to how old I was and in what grade, and – most of all – how much we loved him and were taking care of him.

"Daddy, I'm seven years old now. If you love me, squeeze your eyes tight," and he would.

"Daddy, I'm going to junior high now. If you love me, squeeze your eyes tight," and he did.

Then, as quickly and as unannounced as he had entered our world, he would slip back into a world we were not aware of nor ever able to visit.

"Don't be afraid, because you will not be ashamed. Don't be embarrassed, because you will not be disgraced. You will forget the shame you felt earlier; you will not remember the shame you felt when you lost your husband. **The God who made you is like your husband.** *His name is the Lord All-Powerful. The Holy One of Israel is the one who saves you. He is called the God of all the earth."*
Isaiah 54:4-5 (NCV, emphasis mine)

True to His Word, the Lord honored Mom, giving her grace and favor with many who came in contact with her. At times, God downright spoiled her. Mom had homes and cars distinctly given to her by God. One can imagine the financial condition we were in, and yet a minister friend of ours once stated, "Rita always looks like a million dollars."

One of my favorite childhood memories of God's favor over Mom is when she told the Lord, "Gee, Lord, before he got sick, Peter always gave me flowers. I never get flowers anymore."

That month, bouquets from all over the place came to our home. Flowers by the dozens filled every room in our house. These bouquets fragranced our home with not only their beautiful aroma, but with the scent of the presence of God. It was a physical reminder of Matthew 6:28-30. If He cares for the lilies of the field, how much *more* does He care for us?

We couldn't imagine in those early years what God's plans for our lives would look like. Still, we knew it would consist of holding on to His Word and promises that, no matter what came our way, His plans were not meant to harm us. His plans consisted of a future where we could hope and believe that, as we called out to God, He would listen to us. Our lives would consist of growing up seeking God with all our heart – even during the dark days ahead – knowing He would always be found.

LARVA STAGE

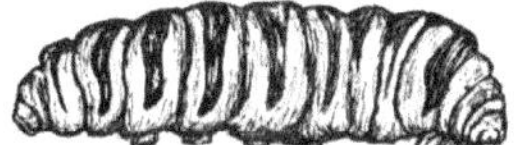

The female butterfly covers her eggs with a nutritious coating as she lays them. Some caterpillars actually eat their egg cases. Once they emerge from the egg, caterpillars are like an eating machine, only resting to digest their food. They race against other caterpillars on the plant as well as against armies of ants, birds, and parasitic wasps that search them out.

Caterpillars don't have a skeleton. In order for them to grow, they shed their skins four or five times in their life. A freshly-hatched caterpillar will grow one thousand times its own weight in just three weeks. Butterflies spend the majority of their lives as a caterpillar. If a butterfly were a person, it would still be a caterpillar at age sixty.

"Don't count out your seasons because the sky of the future looks better than the soil of today. You learn to appreciate the flowers and clouds as a butterfly once you've been in the leaves and dirt as a caterpillar."

~ Karissa Leiann

Chapter Two

KNOW THE GOD OF YOUR FATHER

"And you, my son Solomon, acknowledge the God of your father, and serve Him with wholehearted devotion and with a willing mind, for the LORD searches every heart and understands every motive behind the thoughts. If you seek Him, He will be found by you."
1 Chronicles 28:9

Every morning, I woke up at 5:00 a.m. to the sound of Nana's rolling pin rhythmically dragging across the cutting board to make fresh tortillas. *Every* morning.

When Dad first came home from the hospital, Mom tried to rent an apartment, take care of my dad, and raise me all by herself. Unsurprisingly, the burden proved too difficult, so the three of us moved in with my Nana and Tata, Basilio and Rosario Lopez, at their home in Fullerton. Nana filled each early morning with homemade flour tortillas and the smell of refried beans, bacon, and potatoes.

My Tata was my main father figure. He provided the stability and strength I needed in my life. Having lost his own father at a young age, he taught me how to ride my bike, how to spit the right way, and, in the summer, he took me swimming at the community center every day. He faithfully drove me to school, took me on adventures throughout the community, showed me how to find a bargain, and taught me from the many wise things he had taught himself.

We lived exactly two blocks from the same church where Mom had first seen Dad and where Dad had been a youth leader. On Sundays, Nana and I woke up early, dressed in our Sunday best, and walked to church at 8:30 a.m. She would say hello to everyone she saw along the way and invite them to church. Almost every time, they declined – some even hid – but she always promised to keep them in her prayers.

Nana was a deaconess at our church, and she was among the first to arrive before the service started to kneel at her bench and pray. We always sat in the back row on the right-hand-side of the church where she could welcome every member, pray during the service, and keep an eye on all the kids – especially the ones chewing bubble gum.

Tata used to stay home on Sundays and watch the televangelists until, one day, I commented it would be better for him to come in person with Nana and me, instead. That next Sunday, we three started riding to church in Tata's car.

As a kid, I was sometimes embarrassed when Nana would quietly slip out of her seat, walk up to the teenagers, and tell them to stop talking during the preaching, or when Tata would give his opinion as to how things should run at church, solicited or not. But my grandmother was the first one to take those same teenagers to the altar, ask them if they would like to accept Jesus Christ as their personal Lord and Savior, and lead them in the Sinner's Prayer while great big tears rolled down their cheeks. They would hug and thank her for caring. And, more often than not, Tata was *right* about the things he suggested.

Mom always attended the 11:00 a.m. Sunday service. She spent the mornings getting me ready to go with my grandmother, then getting Dad ready for the day, and finally dressing herself for church. Dad's routine consisted of bathing and shaving him, brushing his teeth, feeding him through the G-tube in his stomach, changing the dressings that surrounded the hole in his abdomen, and splashing him with cologne. Until I was old enough to dress myself, Mom took care of getting us both ready, and my daddy and I always looked perfect.

Upon her arrival to church, Mom would take her place at the piano where she stayed until the sermon began. When one of the members went long during testimony time, she was very good at playing a little something as a cue to wrap things up. I loved when Mom would signal for me to join her at the altar. I would climb up on the bench beside her and she'd tell me which piano keys to play to complement the chords she was playing during the congregational singing. It was almost like playing a duet!

As a true daughter of my Nana, Mom kept a close eye on *me* during the service, and if I was talking or laughing with my friends, I would glance up at her to check if she had seen me. All while keeping her eyes on the sheet music, Mom would put a pleasant grin on her face, nod her head up and down that she *had* seen me, and make a quick gesture with her right hand that let me know I was going to get a spanking if I didn't behave. I'm not sure if anyone caught it but me, but boy did it send chills down my spine. I learned at an early age to be reverent in the house of the Lord.

Those church members who knew my dad before he became ill would share stories with me about what he was like.

"Your dad was such a good preacher!"

"I remember your dad playing bass and piano."

"Man, your dad sure did love Jesus."

"I remember when your dad . . ."

I relished and welcomed all the stories I could hear, and I fantasized how I would place all those unknown pieces into a *known* dad who had, at one time, existed outside of the hospital bed where he currently lay. One underlying current of the many facets of my dad remained consistent in those stories: Dad *loved* God!

My whole family loved God, and each person revealed to me a characteristic of God that taught *me* to love Him on their level. I watched my parents and grandparents wholeheartedly serve God with an unwavering devotion, despite what we all were going through. I listened as they sought the Lord for wisdom on how to proceed throughout their daily lives, being mindful that they walked according to God's Word. I came to learn how to balance spirit-led stirrings of the heart with logical understanding of God-given knowledge. I saw my family remain steadfast in the Lord. As these four role models God had placed in my home journeyed with Him, I learned and followed suit.

I came to know the God of my father *and* my mother, my grandfather *and* my grandmother. Their motives to raise me in a godly home guided their actions, and their love for God caused me to seek out that same love for myself.

Chapter Three

FOR MY WAYS ARE NOT YOUR WAYS

"'For My thoughts are not your thoughts, neither are your ways My ways,'
declares the Lord. For as the heavens are higher than the earth, so are My
ways higher than your ways and My thoughts than your thoughts."
Isaiah 55:8-9

When I was around seven years old, we took Dad to a big healing service like the ones you hear about from the days of the great revivals. It was late in the day and Mom had never taken Dad out of the house except to the hospital. She had been convinced by someone from church to take him *there* to be healed.

I wanted to go, but I was supposed to stay at home with Nana and Tata. I was quiet as I watched Mom prepare to leave with Dad. I normally didn't ask for anything because somehow I knew I shouldn't be a burden. I was also afraid of being rejected by being told no.

But *this* was important. I wanted to go. My heart burned so badly because I *needed* to go. *What if he is healed? I won't be there!* And so, I found the courage to ask.

Mom must have been surprised to see the pleading in my eyes, how determined I was. I'm sure she could see a piece of me would die if she went without me. She said yes!

Mom and Nana got me ready quickly, putting me in one of the dresses I always wore to church. They gave me two pigtails shaped into Shirley Temple curls, each with a pink cotton bow. I wore a white blazer and white knee-high socks with white sandals.

It was nighttime and tons of people came into our home to gently load Dad into the back of a van. I sat by his side as street lights whooshed by. Dad shook his head from side to side, moaning at what was unfamiliar.

He couldn't communicate verbally, and we never knew how much he understood, but he would moan and shake his head when he needed something or was uneasy. Sometimes it seemed like he did it without reason. Maybe it was just to know he still could.

Gosh, it embarrassed me when friends came over and he did that. They would ask if they could "see" my dad or I would watch them slowly walk past his room so they could catch a glimpse of him. He wasn't something to "see." He was just my daddy and all I knew at the time was that he had gotten a very bad illness and now his brain was somehow damaged. I imagine it sounded scary to someone who didn't know what that moaning noise was, especially in the middle of the night. I hardly had friends come over because, while it was normal for us, I didn't know what they would think. I didn't want to have to answer prying questions of which not even I was sure of the answers.

Dad especially moaned when he was hungry. We fed him every four hours through the tube in his stomach. Two cans of Ensure and two cans of water. Every four hours. That schedule ruled our lives. We did almost everything in four-hour increments. We went to church and were back within four hours. We went to the store and were back within four hours.

Sometimes, when the Ensure accidentally spilled out of the tube and onto Dad's stomach, his skin would get raw and we would have to clean it with 4x4 bandages and apply some type of medicated ointment. I was little and was taught to feed my dad through the tube in his stomach. It wasn't my job all the time, but I did it when I needed to help out.

On the night of the great healing service, I looked at the blankets draped over my dad and knew we had four hours until he would need to be fed. I remember thinking how weird it would be if others saw Mom feed Dad with the extra cans of Ensure that were in her bag.

Kneeling beside my moaning dad in the back of the van, I put my hand on his arm in an attempt to comfort him. Finally, we stopped. There was a flurry of people and lights in the darkness of the street as we got out of the van and took him into Angeles Temple.

Someone was mindful of me and held my hand; I don't remember who, but it wasn't Mom. We went inside and placed Dad on a makeshift cot on top of some chairs turned around to create a bed. Mom brushed Dad's hair, put Vaseline on his lips, and put a little bit of blush on his face so he wouldn't look pale or sickly. She didn't want everyone who helped carry my six-foot tall dad to think he smelled, so at home she had given him a good bath and put cologne on him.

We stood around at the church and waited. Mom's best friend, Rosie, who loved to read and had taught me how to silently read "in my head," had her camera with her. She told me to stand by my dad so she could take a picture. She might have done it to keep me entertained, or she might have done it because of what was going on. I don't know, but what I do know is that she took a picture that would forever be the emblem of my faith, the source of my pain, and the symbol of hope throughout my life still to this day.

I stood next to Dad with one knee-high sock slightly higher than the other, and I smiled as best as I could. In my little heart, I knew I needed to be strong. I wanted my daddy to see in the picture that I had the faith that helped him get healed that night. When Dad got out of that bed, I wanted him to see I had been brave. So, I smiled my best smile. He didn't shake his head, as if he knew to keep still for the picture.

A long time passed. Someone took me by the hand and we sat down with the rest of the people in the auditorium while Mom waited at the side of the stage with the others who would help her take Dad to the altar for prayer. I waited and waited and drew on the paper in the pocket of the seat in front of me. I was given gum to chew, and I waited. It couldn't have been long; then again, maybe it was. Regardless, it seemed like forever.

Suddenly I heard someone say, "There goes your daddy!"

I stood up and careened my neck to see him, but I couldn't. I heard people gasping and I tried to see, but I saw nothing. He was getting healed and I couldn't see!

Then I heard mumbling and murmuring and tones of complaint, all hushed so I wouldn't hear. A long time of more waiting.

Then Mom came over to us.

"Let's go," she said.

"But what happened? What's going on? What did they tell you?" All these questions in my own mind were also asked by the adults all around me.

Silence.

We got back in the van and I watched my dad shake his head some more. Side to side, side to side.

Did he eat? Why didn't God heal him?

I fell asleep on the ride home to whispers all around me, explanations I'd never heard. I felt that I was carried into the house, dressed in pajamas, and placed into bed with a kiss on my forehead.

One day, I would understand why God did what He did.

Chapter Four

CALL TO ME, AND I WILL ANSWER YOU

*"Call to Me and I will answer you, and will tell you great
and hidden things that you have not known."*
Jeremiah 33:3

I knew from a very young age what my mission in life had to be. I needed to get my dad *healed* and then everything would be as it should. All throughout my childhood, I heard the stories of Jesus healing the blind man and the leper. Jesus even raised Lazarus from the dead. Jesus was *my* Jesus too, and if He could do that for them, He could do it for me.

I asked Jesus into my heart after a guest speaker preached about the rapture. We went to a very Pentecostal church where altar calls meant everyone went up for prayer regardless of their condition or need. The kids would pray for a little while and then go back to their seats to talk or draw on pieces of paper while the adults praised Jesus and were filled with the Holy Spirit.

But that night, after hearing about God's return, Mom found me crying and asked what was wrong. I told her I was scared.

"I don't want to go to hell; I want to go to heaven."

Mom prayed the Sinner's Prayer with me and I asked Jesus into my heart. I was only five.

Mom sent me to my first Missionette Camp in Idyllwild, California when I was nine years old. Missionettes, now called *Girls Ministries*, is a Christian program that closely resembles Girl Scouts in community service and merit badges, but also includes Scripture reading and memorization. It was exciting to be away with all the other girls, stay in a cabin, sleep in a bunk bed, and walk to the bathrooms to take cold showers. That first night changed my life forever.

Reverend Delia Mora was the women's ministry director for the Pacific Latin American District of the Assemblies of God and also oversaw the Missionettes. On the first night, she told all of us young girls that Jesus wanted to touch our hearts and that Holy Spirit would fill us with the gift of speaking in tongues. Girls everywhere – some my same age, some older and younger – were praising God, singing, raising their hands, and even speaking in tongues just like the adults in our church. What I saw made me realize Jesus was for everyone, no matter how old we were! He wanted to touch all our lives. I knew beyond any doubt that I was standing in God's presence with all the other little girls. I began to cry at how real I could feel God's love in my heart.

Within a few days, I found myself raising my arms, praising God, and speaking in tongues. I felt God's love and power, and I knew – even stronger than before – that, if He wanted to, He could heal my dad. Sitting quietly on my bunk, I thanked God for loving me and asked Him to please heal my dad. I prayed that when I got home, Dad would be there waiting for me, completely healed.

The rest of that week was filled with days of swimming, crafts, sports, devotions, and nights of worship where we praised Jesus and experienced Him to the fullest.

On the ride home, I grew more and more excited that God had healed my dad just as I had asked him to. When we arrived at church, I ran to

Mom and gave her a big hug. I looked around for Dad, but he wasn't there. *They must want to surprise me when I get home,* I thought.

I pictured Dad in a brown suit, sitting in a chair in his room with his legs crossed and a Bible on his lap. I'm not sure where I came to the conclusion that he was supposed to look like that, but in my nine-year-old mind, that's what I imagined.

I ran inside the house to his room, but he wasn't in his chair. He was still in his hospital bed. Nothing had changed even the slightest about him.

Disappointed, I walked to my room and sat on my bed. I asked God *why* He didn't heal my dad. He didn't tell me.

I decided to create a plan to earn God's favor so He would heal my dad. I was already a pretty obedient kid and didn't have any brothers or sisters to fight with, so I had to think of what sin was keeping God from healing Dad. All I could think of was that I didn't *always* obey Mom as I should, and occasionally (*very often*) I told "white lies" about things. I promised God that I would be obedient and never lie ever again for the rest of my life so that He would heal my dad.

Well, being obedient only lasted a few weeks and lying was a constant issue, so I promised God I would obey and not lie for *five* years. I'm not sure how long I lasted that time around, but I found myself changing my promise from five years, to one year, to ten months, until I finally saw that there was no way I could be sinless – much less be able to sin *less* – for any amount of time that would merit God healing my dad. I decided I would read my Bible, pray, and be the best I could so God would see my efforts and eventually decide. One time, I even told God I would switch places with my dad, asking God to let *me* be the sick one and let Dad be well again.

Throughout my life, I always had three questions for God. I constantly asked God, *Why did you let Dad get sick?* Surely there were worse people that deserved to get sick such as criminals, sinners, and bad people. The second was, *When will you heal my dad?* It wasn't a question of *if* but *when,* because I knew He would. My last question was established later in my teens: *Will you please let my dad speak to me before he dies?* Those questions stayed in my heart and I patiently waited for Him to answer.

While I was singing in the choir at church in my twenties, the pastor stopped and asked for those who needed healing to put their hand over that particular area while he prayed.

In my spirit, I heard Holy Spirit tell me, *Put your hand on your heart.*

I questioned Him, but then I obeyed. A small hole in my heart was revealed that needed to be filled in order for me to be whole. As I reached up to put my hand on my heart, I felt God's presence over me so strongly that I had to get down from the platform to go pray in a corner of the altar.

As I kneeled there, sobbing, the Lord told me, *Ask Me.*

I then realized what He was telling me to ask. But I hadn't gotten an answer my entire life, and now it hurt too much to think of asking Him again only to find out He wasn't going to give me an answer.

Ask Me.

No, Lord, I don't want to ask. I don't need to know, I prayed. *I trust You and that's all that matters.*

Ask Me.

No, please don't make me ask You, I cried. *Every time I've asked, You've never responded. As a child, it hurt my heart when You refused to heal my daddy and even more so that You wouldn't explain to me why. As an adult who has seen Your faithfulness over all these years, I don't need to know. I'm* fine.

Then, an assuring feeling came over me as He whispered again to my heart, *Ask Me.*

I knew I was going to get an answer this time. *Why, Lord,* why *did you let my dad get sick? Why* him*? Why not someone else?*

And the answer came in only four words and nothing else: *Because he was willing.* That was it.

What an impact! Such a simple, profound answer.

To some degree, I already knew that, but somehow I didn't *know that.* It was as if I had been seeing something through dirty glass and now I understood completely. God allowed my dad to get spinal meningitis simply because Dad had asked that God would use him to the fullest. No matter what it was, Dad was willing. In no way am I saying that God *gave* my dad spinal meningitis, rather, that God – in His sovereignty and omniscience – knew the greater picture of it all. Instead of healing my dad, He used our lives through the illness as a means of reaching others to reveal God's love *in* and *despite* our circumstances.

What an honor to know my dad loved God and God's people so much he was willing to be used by God in any way, shape, or form. Whether from the pulpit preaching out loud, or in a hospital bed as a silent witness for thirty-two years, my dad was willing.

It was a great revelation, and my heart swelled with the honor of being part of such a strategic and purposeful plan of God. And then I questioned myself. Was *I* willing to do whatever God asked of me?

"For we are His workmanship, created in Christ Jesus for good works,
which God prepared **beforehand***, that we should walk in them."*
Ephesians 2:10, emphasis mine

Chapter Five

EL ROI

"So she called the name of the LORD who spoke to her, 'You are a God of seeing,' for she said, 'Truly here I have seen Him who looks after me.'"
Genesis 16:13

I remember the first time Mom yelled for me to come to Dad's room. I was so scared something bad had happened.

When I heard, "Judy, come quickly; your daddy is *awake*," I was relieved. I questioned why *that* was a big deal, and then I thought a miracle had happened.

As she spoke with Dad, I expected him to gain consciousness and eventually be completely restored, ready to live life with us as a healed man.

He did not.

Back at the hospital, when it had been determined Dad had too much brain damage to ever recover, Mom told him, "Peter, if you give me a kiss, I'll take you home."

In the lost abyss of uncertainty of what he did and did not comprehend, that would be her sign that he was still *there* – somewhere there in his senses, somehow still with her.

For a good while in the hospital, he never responded. But one day, Mom walked in and Dad puckered his lips for a kiss – her signal to take him home!

Mom always had faith God could heal Dad. On the first Easter home after his incident, Mom dressed Dad up in a suit, believing the same power that raised Jesus from the dead was the same power able to heal my dad. It did not. She never gave up hope.

When Mom called me over to see Dad "awake" at home for the first time, I believe Mom must have asked my dad the same question, still hanging on to faith as she had other times unsuccessfully. Only, this time, he responded. That day, Mom told him to give her a kiss and he attempted to pucker his lips. I then watched in amazement as she told him to squeeze his eyes tight if he loved us . . . And he did!

I recall the feeling of hope rising up inside me that maybe, just maybe, things were going to change. And then, suddenly, he stopped responding and went away.

I wasn't sure how to feel. An aggressive battle within me surged as I felt the pain of losing him all over again against the hope that he was aware of me, that he, in a sense, *saw* me. That was at least *something*. Still, I was left with no way of knowing when or if it would happen again.

Sometimes, I would go into his room all on my own and talk to him, wishing he'd respond, nonetheless hoping he could somehow hear me or understand what I was saying.

"Daddy, life is really hard right now. I wish you could get better and help us. Couldn't you please ask God to heal you?"

I never knew if he relayed the message.

We never knew what or how much Dad understood. The doctors had told Mom that he had become blind, but we also knew if he could hear us, his other senses would be much stronger. If we painted pictures with our words, then perhaps, in some way or another, he really could see us.

The only video I have of my dad as a well man is from my parents' wedding. It was shot without light, so the inside videos are very dark. Because it's recorded from a reel, the video skips and jumps a lot. There's one small glimpse of him standing outside, a mere thread to a greater woven tapestry I was never able to grasp. It's the only time I ever saw him well. Mere seconds on poorly developed film was all I was given in life.

When I was a little girl, Mom tried to style my big curly hair like Diana Ross or coil my hair around her finger to look like Shirley Temple. I have almond-shaped eyes and, at times, people questioned my nationality. I always figured I could go into almost any country and people just might believe I was one of them!

A birthmark the size of my thumb sits on the left side of my face, just along my jawline. Interesting questions along with some labels often plagued me as a kid. It didn't help that I was skinny and really tall for being hispanic. *Judy* rhymes with many things, and kids are so "creative."

Navigating all parts of my identity without a healthy, traditional, relationship with a dad was difficult; however, I always held on to the knowledge that my name was on Dad's lips when his high fever had him hallucinating. It gave me an idea of how much he loved me.

I wish I had been old enough to remember my dad saying my name. Three months isn't any time at all to get to know someone, much less when you *are* three months old. I was never able to experience what Dad was like – his mannerisms, the sound of his voice, or what he would have taught me throughout life.

In my hunger to know God more, to discover this God whom my dad loved so much and my mom trusted so much, I read the whole Bible over and over again. I wanted to know Him for *myself.*

I came across a story in Genesis 16 about a slave who was used, mistreated, and then sent away to die with her son in the desert wilderness. She was a nobody, and yet God *saw* her. Regardless of her condition, regardless of whether or not she was *worthy* to be seen.

God saw her. Then He rescued her.

As I read that story, I learned she gave God a name – a name personal and special to her, a name I had never heard or seen before.

In Genesis 16:13, she called God *El Roi,* or "the God who sees me."

God sees *me*!

*"Before I formed you in the womb **I knew you**, and before you were*
born I consecrated you; I appointed you a prophet to the nations."
Jeremiah 1:5, emphasis mine

Not just the whole, round world with billions of people who look like ants scattering around busily, confused when someone disturbs the path. God sees and knows us *individually.*

Singularly.

Personally.

"But you, O Lord, know me; You see me, and
test my heart toward You."
Jeremiah 12:3a

He's concerned and interested in every detail of our lives. He sees our thoughts that rummage through the secret recesses of our minds and cause us sleepless nights.

He sees our heart and those things that make it beat uncontrollably at various intervals. God reminds our soul that things are going to be okay. He's completely aware of us because He truly *sees* us.

> *"The eyes of the LORD search the whole earth in order to*
> ***strengthen*** *those whose hearts are fully committed to Him."*
> 2 Chronicles 16:9a (NLT, emphasis mine)

Chapter Six

BY HIM WE CRY, ABBA FATHER

"But when the fullness of time had come, God sent forth his Son, born of woman, born under the law, to redeem those who were under the law, so that we might receive **adoption as sons***. And because you are sons, God has sent the Spirit of his Son into our hearts, crying, 'Abba! Father!' So you are no longer a slave, but a son, and if a son, then an heir through God."*
Galatians 4:4-7, emphasis mine

Throughout my childhood, I had my ups and downs; but in general, life was good. God showed Himself faithful by surrounding me with people who rose up to mold and shape me. Overall, my childhood was amazing.

Then, I became a teenager.

My world was upside-down internally as a teen, and I didn't need any help from the outside world that couldn't care less if I was ready for what it had in store. First, my oldest childhood friend, Martha, moved away. Then, my best friend and dearest sister to my heart, Maricela, moved when we were in junior high. I lost another great friend when the pastors I had grown up with and their daughter were called to pastor another church. More of my church friends moved away. A family in our church created a split, and we lost many members. I tried to restructure my life and attended a separate youth group from our church only to discover everyone was so much younger than I was. Surviving junior high was a story all on its own.

Overall, it was a difficult time in my life. So I did the only thing I had control over: I prayed.

For some reason, Dad's room was always a peaceful place. I frequented it to listen to my storybook records and read. My Nana and I always suspected Jesus came and visited my dad in there when we weren't home. We knew that room was anointed. Nana kneeled and prayed every evening beside an old, cozy burnt-orange chair in a corner of Dad's room.

From my bedroom next to his, I would hear Nana's prayers for her kids and grandkids, for the pastor and missionaries, and for the unsaved people she knew. She'd pray for my dad's healing, and I regularly heard her call my name out to God. Nana praised God and worshiped Him during those evenings.

I knew Nana brought down God's presence into Dad's room every night. I figured that chair where she prayed must be anointed. When Nana finished praying and left Dad's room, I would quickly slip right in and kneel by that chair to pray, hoping to catch God's presence before it left.

One particular evening, I'd had a bad day and really needed to talk to God. It seemed as if everything that could go wrong at home, church, and school had. I remember telling God that, if I had my dad, everything would be as it should. But it wasn't. That night, I dared to tell God He had made a mistake by allowing my dad to get sick.

As I complained to God, I heard Him in my heart tell me to get up and lay hands on Dad. The realization of what God was telling me stunned me. God was going to give me what I had always wanted: a daddy. And not only that, but God was going to use *me* to heal my dad!

40

The lights were off in his room and I could see the moon shining through slits in the miniblinds. Dad no longer needed to be fed every four hours with Ensure through his G-tube; modern medical technology allowed him to be continuously fed through a feeding machine that looked similar to an I.V. We still lived in four-hour increments because Mom had to return home to turn him from his side to his back and vice versa so he wouldn't get bed sores. The *only* time Dad ever got a bed sore was during an extended hospital stay after they relocated his G-tube. The hospital staff wasn't as diligent as Mom, and *we* ended up turning him during his hospital stay as well.

In the quiet of the room, the only noise was the soft humming of the machine and distant sounds of my family getting ready for bed. I walked slowly toward Dad, imagining him getting up from his bed and giving me a big hug. I pictured yelling for Mom and my grandparents to come and witness the miracle.

I approached Dad's hospital bed, wondering if I should place my hand on his head because of the brain damage or over his heart, the essence of who he was. I chose the latter and placed my hand on his heart. Nothing happened. I sobbed at the feeling of rejection that flooded over me. *God* had rejected my request. *Do I not have enough faith?*

For some reason, I felt humiliated by the whole thing. Did God not love me? What did I do wrong? I know I *felt* I had heard God right. I thought I had enough faith. Surely this whole crazy life we were living was for a reason . . . A bigger plan? A purpose? *Something?*

All of a sudden, the room became bright and I was hugged from behind by a strong, warm embrace. I turned around, expecting to find Nana by the light switch. I assumed she had seen everything and was now hugging me. But there was no one in the room!

At that moment, I felt God's presence tightly wrap around me, and I clearly heard the Lord tell me:

All your life, you've wanted your dad. It's the only thing you've really asked for with all your heart. You want your dad? I give you a dad. I give you . . . Me. I AM your dad. I will always love you and take care of you. I will protect you and guide you. I'll provide for your every need. I AM your dad. Other dads let their kids down; other dads disappoint their kids; other dads are never there for their kids; other dads leave their kids and don't care for them. I will never leave you. I will never let you down. I will never disappoint you. I will never beat you. You want your dad? I AM your dad.

And that was it.

I cried and cried because it seemed God was telling me no, that he wouldn't heal my dad. Then I cried even more at the realization that God loved me enough to make His presence real in my life by literally hugging me, speaking to me, and assuring me that *He* would be the perfect dad I needed.

When Moses saw the burning bush he asked God, "Who can I say you are?" God's reply was, "I AM that I AM." And so it is to this day. God assured my dad of that very thing when He audibly told him, "Times have changed but I AM still the same."

God promised me that very same thing when He told me, *I AM your dad.* Whatever questions we can ask of God, whatever we need from God, whatever we need God to be in our lives at that moment, all we ever have to do is ask. His faithful reply will always be, "I AM," because all His promises in the Bible are *yes* and *amen*!

After that night, I never asked God to heal my dad again. I knew I didn't need to. If He wanted to, He would and could. But if not, I had

Him. He was my Abba Father, the term the Hebrew children gave to describe God as *Daddy.*

Not long after that remarkable evening, I found this verse in Romans and held on tightly to His promise:

For all who are led by the Spirit of God are sons of God. For you did not receive the spirit of slavery to fall back into fear, but you have received the Spirit of adoption as sons, by whom we cry, **"Abba! Father!"** The Spirit himself bears witness with our spirit that we are children of God, and if children, then heirs – heirs of God, and fellow heirs with Christ, provided we suffer with him in order that we may also be glorified with him.

Romans 8:14-17, emphasis mine

From that night on, God was my Daddy. From that night on, I called Him *Abba.*

Chapter Seven

HE CONSIDERED ME FAITHFUL

*"I thank Christ Jesus our Lord, who has given me strength, that
He considered me faithful, appointing me to His service."*
1 Timothy 1:12

The last Missionette Camp I attended was in 1987 when I was twelve. I had just been baptized the month before and was feeling a sense of purpose and direction. Our pastor had a fantastic philosophy that, once baptized, everyone should serve at church in whatever capacity they were able. He encouraged each of us to find our place, where we fit, in serving at church. I was given a small class of four-year-olds to teach on Sundays, and I loved it.

Mom and her siblings were raised Catholic until they attended a Vacation Bible School held by the local Assemblies of God church in Calexico, California. A simple gesture of inviting some kids from the neighborhood to have punch and cookies at church changed Nana and Tata's life too, resulting in multiple generations being saved.

I enjoyed knowing I was given such an awesome responsibility to make a big difference in these children's lives each Sunday, perhaps the way my own family was changed by children's ministries. I prided myself in studying God's Word, preparing my lessons, and carefully tearing out pictures of Jesus blessing the children on fuzzy flannel board sheets. Every Sunday, I walked into church with my "carpet bag of ministry" to the smiling faces of sweet little kids who couldn't pronounce my English name, Judy. They respectfully called me *Hermana Beauty*, or "Sister Beauty" much to my teenage heart's delight.

I sat in chapel at my last Missionette Camp, planning how I was going to race everyone else to the game room to get my spot at the air hockey table.

To my surprise, a young lady was called up to speak to our group of over three hundred girls. She was the Miss Y of 1987. The "Y" stood for "young women," and this was the teen version that served as the transition group from Missionettes to Women's Ministries. These competitions were similar to the Miss America pageant, but without the bathing suit competition. After preparing herself biblically and competing against others in Bible knowledge, this young lady had earned the crown and privilege of carrying the Miss Y title for the year.

For the rest of us young girls, she served as a role model of what a young woman of God looked like, filled with the Holy Spirit, full of grace and wisdom, and the portrait of what it meant to have a "good testimony." However simple the whole event was, Miss Y was someone to look up to and respect for her achievements.

She opened her Bible and began to preach. I sat in complete reverence of the whole persona she portrayed and the power with which she shared God's Word. Not more than six years older than me, Miss Y was ministering to other young ladies, touching their hearts and allowing God to use her to change their lives.

I found my heart telling the Lord, *I would love to be able to minister to others just like her, but I don't know what I would speak about.*

The Lord responded, *Your dad,* and that was it.

I was shocked by how clearly I had heard Him. The way He said it was kind of like a command. I searched my heart and tried to shut out the sounds around me in order to hear more of what God had to say regarding my dad, wondering *what* about my dad He wanted me to speak about, but I didn't hear anything else.

That night, I spoke in tongues I had never spoken in before.

Five years later, God told me exactly what He meant that night. In my senior year of high school, I submitted my application to Southern California College, the Christian Assemblies of God college in Costa Mesa, now known as Vanguard University. I had applied for grants and scholarships and was well on my way.

But, just before going to college in August of 1993, I attended a youth convention. While I was there, I asked the Lord what He wanted to do with my life. My intentions were to become a pediatrician, but something didn't seem right. I asked my Abba Daddy what *He* wanted from me in regard to my future. God reminded me of that Missionette Camp when I told Him I wanted Him to use me through preaching, but felt I didn't have anything special to preach about. He brought back to my memory the moment He told me, *Your dad.*

During the convention's prayer time at the altar, God asked me, *What do you want to do?*

I want You to use me to tell others about You, I told Him.

He replied, *What do you need to do to be able to tell others about Me?*

Well, I said in my heart, *I need to learn the Bible really well, and I need to learn how to preach.*

Then the Lord, my Abba, told me to go to LABI College, the Bible college my parents had gone to.

My heart sank. I couldn't believe it. While I knew its sole purpose was to train and prepare men and women for full-time ministry, it was so small and nothing like the great universities I had imagined myself attending. I felt like so many people expected great things from me and I might let them down, but there was nothing else I wanted more in life than to be fully used by God.

At that time, LABI College didn't offer scholarships, grants, or any kind of government assistance. My family and I lived off of social security because Mom stayed home to care for Dad. There was no way she could pay for my school, so I told God, *My dad would have paid for my school if he were well. Since You're my dad, if You want me to go to this school, You need to pay for it.* While I said those things respectfully to Him, I had the utmost confidence that if this were truly His plan for my life, He would make a way.

When I got home from the youth convention, I told Mom that I felt God wanted me to go to LABI College. I expected her to be disappointed. Instead, I saw her eyes water with joy from her heart and she gave me a big hug and told me she was proud of me.

I submitted my application and was accepted, but still had no way of paying for it. My pastor at the time lived on LABI's campus and came with some very good news for us. The school board had reviewed my application. Knowing my mom and dad's testimony, they had decided to pay *all* of my schooling – tuition, room, and board. My Abba Father had indeed paid for my schooling. My path was secured and *He* had made sure of it!

I learned so much my first semester, the greatest being how to speak in front of others. I had been in church plays all my life and performed in singing, piano, and other musical competitions. But, for some reason, speaking in front of the class my first semester was a nightmare. I would get so nervous and forcefully yawn to the point of tears streaming from my eyes while butterflies frantically fluttered inside my stomach and up my throat. It was awful!

Although I always got A's on my quizzes and tests, I could not get a decent speech out of my mouth. Many times, I just fumbled through the whole thing, *if* I finished at all.

A classmate told me that I was smart, but it was too bad I couldn't speak in public. "It's okay," he tried to assure me. "God will use you in another way."

I had a talk with my Abba Daddy about it, and God told me if I was going to preach, I needed to get over my nerves, prepare myself well, and give my best for the final speech of the semester.

I prepared my speech against abortion, printed pictures and pasted them on cardboard, made my points clear, and studied hard so I wouldn't even need my notes. I requested to give my speech first, tricking myself so I would begin speaking *before* the yawning could start and the butterflies could wreak havoc in my stomach.

During my speech, I walked around my class, looking everyone in the eyes, showing them my pictures, and proving my points. I smiled as I took my seat. I knew I had done well.

Final grades were passed out a few weeks later. That one classmate got a B and I got an A, much to *both* of our surprise. Unable to contain himself, he insisted that the teacher explain what seemed to be an error. My wise teacher simply stated that while my classmate spoke really well, he did poorly on his tests. I may have stumbled through speaking, but I got all A's on my tests. When it came down to it, I had *learned* something in the class. I had grown and improved from not being able to speak well at all to presenting a really great speech, and *that* was the point of going to school.

At the start of my second year of Bible school, LABI informed me that, due to finances, the school could only provide for my tuition – not my room and board. I reminded my Abba Father of His promise. A few weeks later, I auditioned and was accepted into our school choir, just as my parents had been. Participating in the school choir meant touring, going to churches to minister, raising funds, and creating awareness for the school. It also meant getting a portion of our tuition paid for. The amount given to us just so happened to equal the exact amount I needed to pay for all my schooling.

Participating in the choir was amazing. I imagined Mom and Dad at the same churches I was singing in. I visited cities and states I had never been to before. My best memory was when we went to the church of someone who had known Dad well. He told me how much he looked up to him. He played me some of the songs Dad and his group used to perform. I was even able to sing with him after church while the musicians jammed, just as I would have with my dad if he was well.

Leading into my third year of Bible school, I was in need of funding again. A female minister had passed away and told her family that in lieu of receiving flowers for her funeral, she wanted the money to go to a young female Bible school student who showed promise, had a calling upon her life, and had a financial need. Our dear friend Reverend Ray Mesa told the family he knew of the perfect girl, and he soon informed me of the blessing I would receive.

For all three years at LABI, I had my schooling paid for by my Abba Father. I also received the occasional ten dollars to wash my clothes, twenty dollars to pay for gas to go home, and special treats from my Aunt Marti.

As I prepared to transfer to Southern California College (SCC) near the end of my third year, I reminded God of His promise to provide for me. My new desire was to be a teacher. Instead of being a pediatrician who healed the bodies of little kids, I wanted to be a children's pastor who showed kids *Who* could heal their heart. I was given the position at our church in Fallbrook to be the children's pastor during my second year. What better vocation for a children's pastor to have than to be a school teacher where all the kids could be found?

With my horrific days of first-year speech class behind me, I finished my time at LABI and was honored to be chosen as our graduating class's valedictorian. I had grown to be well-rounded academically and socially as I was the first-year class president, second-year ASB secretary, and third-year class president. I had also been involved in choir, missions, and evangelism. The Lord had prepared me so well at LABI that when I applied to SCC, more than seventy percent of my tuition was to be paid for.

God had appointed me to His service, seen my faithfulness in chasing after Him wherever He led me, and given me the strength and grace to be successful through it all.

Chapter Eight

REJOICE IN THE WIFE OF YOUR YOUTH

"Rejoice in the wife of your youth."
Proverbs 5:18

I knew God chose José Velazquez for me the day he introduced himself to Dad. I was sixteen and we barely knew each other when he started attending our church. We had invited the youth over for a movie. When it was time to start the film, we could not find José. His car was parked in front of our house, but he was nowhere to be found.

We looked all over the house except for in Dad's room. There was no reason why José should be there, but, as I peeked through the slightly opened door, there José was. I asked him what he was doing there and he just smirked, told me "nothing," and walked past me. I later found out he had introduced himself to my dad as my friend – not knowing whether Dad heard him or not – and promised to take care of me for the rest of our lives. We weren't even dating!

None of my guy friends had ever been intentional about treating my dad with respect and honoring the man of our home like that. The Lord opened my eyes as I began to check off my list of things I had been praying for in a husband. José was my dream come true.

It was interesting to see God's master plan unfold as we compared notes as to where we grew up, what schools we went to, and what friends we had. We found out we both attended the same preschool in Fullerton. I walked with my head down most of that time, so I don't remember seeing José. He says he remembers me in a pink jumper with Shirley Temple curls. My absolute favorite thing to wear was my pink jumper with a strawberry on the pocket. Up until fifth grade, Mom tried her best to brush my curly hair like Shirley Temple every chance she got.

There's a picture of José in kindergarten, carefully drawing on the chalkboard with intense concentration. He says he remembers it well. When asked what he was drawing, he told them a little girl he met. It was a drawing of *me*.

Around the time I was in sixth grade, our church hosted a vow renewal ceremony for the couples of our congregation. Nana and Tata never formally had a wedding ceremony, so this was a big event for our entire family – including their seven children and all of us cousins.

As my cousins and I ran around the church playing tag, Mom stopped me and introduced me to "Elvia's nephew, José." Mom told me to invite him to come play with us.

I asked, and being at the age when you just don't go play with strange boys or girls, he said no. I shrugged and we continued playing without him.

Years later, when we watched a video of that wedding ceremony, for a few precious seconds, we could see little José with slightly bushy, curly hair, chomping away on a piece of bubble gum. Whoever was videotaping at the time caught the little boy who would eventually become the man who made all my dreams come true.

During the time Dad was having his G-tube replaced and we were at the hospital for an extended period of time, Margarita, José, Josue, and

Maggie Velazquez started attending church. I was sixteen at the time, and Nana told me about a handsome young man who had started attending our church.

"He's around your age and very tall," she told me. She hinted that if she were young like me, she would find him very attractive. I pretended I wasn't interested, but couldn't wait to find out who it was.

After those few months in the hospital, Mom and I found ourselves back at church on Easter Sunday. As we watched the traditional Easter play, I made note of which friends were cast as the various characters. One particular Roman soldier jeering at Jesus as he carried his cross toward his death caught my eye.

Who's that guy? I wondered. His Roman mask prevented me from seeing his face but I did notice he had very nice ankles showing beneath that Roman skirt.

As if she knew, Nana leaned over and said, "*That's* José."

Because Dad was still recuperating, we left church immediately following the program and I didn't get to meet José. As we walked down the hall toward our Sunday School classes the following week, I felt someone gently pull my curls. I turned and had to look up to see who it was. I hadn't officially met him, but I knew this gorgeous, six-foot-three guy with the nice ankles had to be José.

But Nana was wrong. He wasn't my age – he was old! He had a mustache, and I figured he had to be twenty-one years old. He followed me to the youth group and I assumed he'd entered the wrong class.

In the weeks that followed, I noticed he would try to bump into me at church, but his age and mustache intimidated me. I would walk the other way or sneak past him through an alternate path at church. Finally, we officially met and started talking more and more. I eventually got up the nerve to ask him his age since he always hung around us younger youth.

His reply was, "Old enough."

Old enough? What did *that* mean? I was already struggling because he seemed so old. How much older did he want to be? When I finally got an answer, I found out he was actually six months *younger* than me! Somehow that lessened the threat and we quickly became best friends, started dating, and I saw José was God's chosen one for my life.

I knew José was the one because I had made a "husband list" when I was eleven years old and prayed over that list every chance I got. It was an idea given to us during a camp break-out session where we were told to take out papers and write down what we wanted in a husband. We were instructed that the first thing at the top of the list had to be "a man of God" and then we could write down whatever else we wanted. My number two was one word: tall.

The Puerto Rican side of me trumped my Mexican side, and I was much taller than most boys I knew. I wanted to wear the tallest high-heeled shoes possible and still have a husband who was taller than me. The rest of my list consisted of things such as someone who was handsome, but not conceited, loved to travel, had a calling over his life, wanted lots of kids, and could help me discover my heritage. I prayed over that list and my person. There were moments I'd pray for his safety and, at times, I'd ask God to give him wisdom. I asked God to give him health, but, most of all, to let him feel God's love.

As our friendship grew, I became aware that José fit exactly what was on my list. I asked God for a sign that José was truly "the one." Not long after, I caught José visiting with Dad. José was mine forever, specifically and especially chosen for me by God. We committed the rest of our lives to one another.

We laugh at it now, but José and I had *three* wedding ceremonies on May 24, 1997. The first was extremely important for me in that we exchanged vows at home in front of Dad. Facing the impossibility of him walking me down the aisle – much less attending any event in person – José and I chose to honor Dad by first seeking his blessing and making our promises to one another in front of him that morning.

Later that afternoon, José and I had our *official* wedding ceremony and reception at The Grand Tradition in Fallbrook. It was a beautiful Victorian mansion with a lake and swans. I had both my paternal and maternal grandfathers walk me down the hill toward the gazebo where José and the rest of our guests waited. Then, just as we had done at my quinceañera, Mom and I walked hand in hand the rest of the way down the aisle as she entrusted me into José's arms on behalf of her and Dad.

I loved everything about our wedding from the mariachi band that serenaded us throughout the entire event, to the rich purple colors decorating the elegant reception, to the delicious wedding cake which had a pistachio top layer – José's favorite – and vanilla with a strawberry and banana filling for the rest, to the many people who loved and celebrated our union.

Immediately following our reception, we headed to church for wedding number three! Our limited financial budget kept us from inviting everyone we knew, so we had to limit our Grand Tradition wedding to only close friends and family. Because we were the children's and youth pastors at our church, our church members wanted to honor us by throwing us a third wedding.

In order to include everyone, we had the kids from church wear white and walk down the aisle as our flower girls and boys. Our remaining bridal party joined us for the second time that day, and we giggled as a different minister led us in wedding vows we had already made twice before.

The *reverence* of our first ceremony was all about honoring my parents. The *elation* of our second ceremony was all about marrying the man of my dreams. The *treasure* of that third ceremony was the memory of my Tío Rick, Tía Gladys's husband, leading me down the aisle.

We left for our honeymoon in Cancún the next day and discovered new worlds as we began our new life together.

CHRYSALIS STAGE

The chrysalis stage is when the caterpillar's miraculous transformation into a butterfly occurs. Inside the chrysalis, huge changes take place where the wings, eyes, tongue, and antennae all develop into new functions. Much of the original caterpillar is turned into a "soup" inside the chrysalis. This nourishes the growth of the new butterfly parts.

The silk wrapping of the chrysalis protects it, keeping the butterfly safe from rain and hidden from predators. Some chrysalises are colored like precious jewels. The word "chrysalis" comes from *khrusos*, the Greek word for "gold."

"Sometimes you need to struggle in the dark for a bit just so you can be stronger when you break into the light. You may feel pressured and broken down, but the process is necessary for your beautiful change to occur."

~ Joseph Peter

Chapter Nine

PURE AND UNDEFILED RELIGION

"Pure and undefiled religion before God the Father is this:
to visit orphans and widows in their affliction, and
to keep oneself unstained from the world."
James 1:27

As a little girl, I was unaware that my home situation was unique. But as I grew up in our small Spanish-speaking church where Mom first caught sight of Dad, I began to notice I was the only one who didn't go home with her daddy. I realized that on Father's Day, while we all colored our papers to give to our daddies, I had to wait until I got home to give my daddy his. As I walked into Dad's room, it hit me that not only could he not hold it or read it, but he could not say how beautiful it was or give me a hug.

One Father's Day at church, we were all handed a letter of the alphabet. Someone had decided at the last minute to have the children read a poem, and I was given one of the letters because of how well I spoke. We were rushed onto the stage. Before I knew it, I was reading words to a father who wasn't there, saying something to the effect of how much I loved having him hold me in his arms. I was little, but somehow I felt embarrassed and humiliated as I read those words out loud.

I dreaded Father's Day after that. Dreaded it to the point of feeling sick to my stomach every year as we rode to church. One year, I made myself so sick that I was able to stay home from church. I tried it again the following year, but when Mom realized what I was doing, she asked why.

I simply told her that while everyone was celebrating with their dads, mine was at home and I'd rather just be home. At church I'd just be talking to someone who wasn't there. She tried to tell me I could still participate because everyone knew my daddy was at home, but my little-girl logic that he couldn't read it or see it was a fact we both had to face.

"Tata loves you like a dad. You can give him your papers and poems," she told me. She was right.

So on Father's Day the following year, back to church I went. Because I was older, we didn't read poems anymore like the little kids did. Boy, was I grateful for that. But the absolute worst, most horrific Father's Day I ever had was when the pastor's wife of our church came into our classroom and told each of us to write down what we liked about our dads.

Believing I was safe, I began to write down everything I had heard *other* people say about my dad: he was kind, he was handsome, he was a great preacher, he played the bass, he loved me, and so on. I actually got carried away and wrote down every single thing I had ever heard about Dad; *none* of which had been experienced firsthand. I began to worry when they collected the papers, but then figured she would give them back to us after church.

All the kids walked into the sanctuary, and each class presented what they had prepared for Father's Day. The littlest ones repeated what they were supposed to. The next class held up their signs and read what their letter meant. All the while I was glad to be past those awful days. But then the pastor's wife stood up and took her place behind the pulpit. In her hands were the sheets I recognized, and she slowly began to read each one.

I convinced myself that, surely, she would not read mine. *What for?* Dad wasn't there to hear it. She *knew* about my dad. She and the pastor had even gone to Bible college with my parents. There was no way she would read it. *No way.*

And then, like a horror story slowly unfolding before me, she held up one last paper. Due to my elaborate descriptions of Dad, I had written all over my page – front and back. As she held up the piece of paper to read what was written, my handwriting glared back at me.

She stated that the paper she held in her hand was the most *special* of all because it was written by a *special* girl who had a *special* father, and she wanted to read it for everyone to hear. As I heard my written words spoken out loud, I sank lower and lower in my seat. Each piercing description of Dad punched a hole into my heart of everything he no longer was. My face was burning hot and my body filled with chills. I saw her lips moving but no longer heard the words. Instead, my ears were filled with the sniffling of church members and muffled sobs of women. I looked around and saw daddies hugging their children a little tighter than usual. They attempted to blink away tears forming in their eyes.

I had not been sitting with Mom; I never did when she played the piano. I sat up and looked around to see her reaction. I wanted to somehow find comfort in her, to catch her winking at me as she always did when she wanted me to know that things were okay. But I could not find her.

I slipped out of my seat and stood at the back of the church so I could better search the congregation for her. I still couldn't see her. My last guess was that she had gone to the bathroom, and I prayed that, by some miracle, she had missed the whole ordeal. I pushed the door open but it was blocked by someone's body. Realizing it was me, the door was opened and I walked into the restroom to discover a group of ladies surrounding someone who was crying. Mom *had* heard the whole thing.

On the worst holiday of the year, I had caused my very own mom pain by reminding her of what once was and now sorrow of what would never be. I was scooted out of the restroom and told everything was "fine," but I knew it wasn't.

I hated myself for that, and I hated that I was placed in that situation in the first place, regardless of their well-meaning intentions.

For many of us growing up without a parent, Father's Day and Mother's Day still hurts. The holidays can cause embarrassment, reminding us we're not whole or that we're lacking something. *Someone.*

In the busyness and "okayness" of their own lives, people forget the widow. They forget the fatherless. But God doesn't. Amazingly, there are those who remember me now – even as an adult – fatherless, but have chosen to step up in their own way to provide a father's love. Their love is a direct result of the prompting from a God who doesn't forget.

> *"And after you have suffered a little while, the God of all grace,*
> *who has called you to His eternal glory in Christ, will Himself*
> ***restore, confirm, strengthen, and establish you.***
> *"*
> 1 Peter 5:10, emphasis mine

I was twenty when Mom and I moved to Fallbrook, California on New Year's Day of 1995. She had been asked to be the assistant pastor of Centro Cristiano de Victoria, and I became the children's pastor as I completed my second year at LABI. A year away from being engaged, José came down on the weekends to serve as the youth pastor. By June, we were accustomed to the new ministries the Lord had placed us in.

On Father's Day, I prepared the kids for their special program for all the daddies in our congregation. Abundantly overjoyed that I was now on *this* side of the spectrum for the annual Father's Day church program, and with a sincere heart, I blindly walked into a horrific scene that I myself had played the star role in during my childhood. Yet this time, *I* was the unsuspecting leader causing unnecessary pain and embarrassment to a young child who was fatherless.

He was an adorable little boy with big brown eyes and curly brown hair. I called out for his father to please stand up to receive his Father's Day card. No one stood up. Once again, I asked for his dad. While I'm sure they made gestures, I did not catch any cues from church members telling me to move on. As I asked one last time for the little boy's daddy to please stand and he didn't, I was told by some not-so-discreet members that his dad wasn't there. I told the boy to give the card to his mom who would take care of it until he got home and could give it to his daddy.

I soon found out that *many* of the other little kids' fathers were also not present. As a matter of fact, more than three-fourths of the kids did not have their daddy present at church that day. With every shake of the head as I read name after name and there was no daddy present, I felt a stab in my own heart as I imagined the pain for that poor child and mother's heart. What's worse is that I didn't even feel I could stop reading names for fear that the few kids who *did* have a daddy there would miss out on the celebration through no fault of their own.

As I walked out of the sanctuary, already so upset at myself, it was made worse when another child whispered to me, "That little boy doesn't have a daddy. His daddy is *dead*."

I went home that night and cried for hours. I cried for myself because I didn't have a daddy. I cried for being so insensitive to the precious kids whose spiritual lives were entrusted into my care, *especially* because I knew how it felt. I cried for the little boy who not only had his father pass away, but had the lady who was in charge of his spiritual well-being publicly humiliate him.

Mom came into the room and let me know that while many of the dads were away because of work, most of those kids whose fathers did not stand up did not have a father waiting for them at home *at all.* A good seventy-five percent of those kids did not have fathers, and I cried to my own Abba Father in sorrow for all of those kids with whom I could relate.

In His gentle and merciful way, the Lord opened my eyes and let me see. I *knew* how they felt. I knew how they felt about being embarrassed in church, but more importantly I knew how they felt when other kids asked them what their daddy did for a living and they couldn't answer. I knew how they felt when they saw other daddies pick up their kids, hug them, tussle their hair, and play with them while their own daddy didn't. I *knew*!

Not only did I know how they felt, but, more importantly, I knew how they *could* feel! Long ago, in a dark room, God had given me a hug and told me that *He* would be my dad. And if He was *my* dad, then, according to the Bible, He was the father of each of those little kids as well. In my heart, I understood that God saw me fit, strong, and faithful enough to allow me to feel that fatherless pain of enduring those dark moments in my life as He shaped me in the chrysalis of His perfect plan for my life . . . *their* lives.

It became so clear that what I had been through was *not* in vain. My unique experience helped me grow to appreciate God, my Abba Father, in a way not many people can. I was able to feel His embrace and hear His words of comfort. I thought back to that time, years ago in my childhood, when I was the only one and it hurt to be in that chrysalis designed just for me. I remembered the times I was lonely and questioned God about His love and why these things were happening to me.

What if it was to help these little kids I now had under my care to see God as *their* Abba Father the way I now did? Could it be? Regardless, I had to be faithful and share my story with them!

I prepared a special lesson for the following Sunday and shared my testimony. I told the children how I was without a daddy, just like them, and how God had hugged me and told me I was His very own. I told them that God was *their* father too and would take care of their every need just as He had taken care of mine.

I understood and found satisfaction knowing everything I had gone through had a purpose. It was up to me to *go* through it, *see* Jesus in it, and *share* it with others to help them. I remembered telling God, *I want to do that . . . but I don't have anything to say.*

Your dad.

I was to share about my dad here on earth *and* about my dad in heaven, my Abba Father.

Chapter Ten

GOD SETS THE LONELY IN FAMILIES

"God sets the lonely in families."
Psalm 68:6a (NIV)

During the years Mom took care of Dad, she also held leadership roles at our church, went to school to educate herself, and took care of me. When she was still in her early thirties, someone joked that Mom had held every position at church except for being the lead pastor and the men's ministry director.

Throughout her life, Mom has always known who her God is, and she's stood faithfully on His Word. She originally only wanted to play the piano, be the wife of a pastor, and raise a large family of her own; but there was another battle planned out for her. As God gave her victory over every obstacle placed in her path, her testimony became the source of encouragement to the many people she personally encountered and others who heard her story.

In 2001, after serving as the assistant pastor of Centro Cristiano de Victoria in Fallbrook for more than six years, Mom was officially elected the lead pastor. She saw her congregation grow and become her extended family with extra brothers and sisters and many, *many* children. While she may not have had a big family the way she intended, Mom *indeed* became a mother of many.

Growing up, I never had biological brothers and sisters like many of my other friends and family did, but God filled my heart. My aunts and uncles stepped up to help raise me, and I had amazing cousins who became like my brothers and sisters.

Undoubtedly, the faith of my family has influenced me greatly. Nana taught me the power of prayer. Completely in love with Jesus, Nana always sang about one day going to Heaven to see Him. She instilled in me the assurance that death was not a bad thing if one only had Heaven to look forward to.

When I was little, Nana would call me over at times to read me a small sermon the Lord had given her. As she spoke, I would look down at her page of notes written in her best penmanship. She would say, "Had I finished school, I would have been a great preacher!" She told me that I would have to preach them for her one day.

Tata taught me to make wise decisions and to practically think things through, balancing thought and ideas in the middle of religiosity. He really did step in as best as he could as a father, helping me purchase my first car, teaching me how to take care of it, and always having wise sayings about life that I live by to this day. Nana and Tata loved me so well!

Tía Linda taught me to listen when God speaks. She gave me the Precious Moments Bible I still carry with me today. Not only have I learned to listen to its words, but I've learned to hear God's voice in the darkness of the night. Tía Linda and Tío Willy were intentional about my spiritual warfare and gave me my love for travel.

Tía Marty was always ready with an open home, a ready meal, and a word of wisdom from the Bible. She was truly my favorite Sunday School teacher, and she helped me see deeper into people and their intentions, believing the best in them and giving people the benefit of the doubt.

Interestingly, I have a second Aunt Marti, and she, along with my Uncle Tony, are also perfect examples of what the gift of hospitality looks like. They consistently took care of Dad, Mom, and me throughout the years in surpassing ways and still hosted others without a home or family. When Psalm 68:6 says, "God places the lonely in families," He is using *them*. These beloved family members showed me the importance of ministering to people's physical needs as well as their spiritual needs.

Tía Rosie resembles Nana in that she's always singing or humming. She reflects God's creative nature in the way she designs everything around her, whether at home or the church she pastors with my Uncle Luis. My love for spray paint, DIY, and using greenery from around the community are all inherited from her.

I always admired Tío Basil's love for his kids as I would hear about him going to their sports games, taking them off-roading, and telling the most incredible stories. Tía Tina and Tío John taught me that effective ministry gets down from the altar, away from the pulpit, and into the crowds with the people as they do life together. To this day, I try to see the world and people through their eyes as they see others through God's eyes.

Dad had one sister, Gladys, and not only has she become the voice of *love* represented from my dad's side of the family, but I truly am a better person because of her. Growing up, she always made sure to include my paternal grandma, Olvido, and uncles Carlos and Ruben into my life. Tía Gladys is the epitome of grace, unconditional love, gentleness, and strength. Whether it's a great find by a small, local store owner or a potential real-estate investment, Tía Gladys can always spot a great deal. She is intentional about being involved in our lives, and I am so grateful because, time after time, she has spoken the words of wisdom I needed to hear into my life.

It truly takes a village to raise a child, and while Mom did an incredible job on her own, I am also blessed with the traces of other lives who stopped along the way to invest in mine. I am who I am, first of all, because of God's mercy and love, and secondly, because of the people He placed in my life. Dad loved God so much that he was willing to be used by Him no matter what that would look like. I see my family doing the same in their own lives throughout their own journey.

"When I call to remembrance the genuine faith that is in you, which dwelt first in your grandmother Lois and your mother Eunice, and I am persuaded is in you also. Therefore I remind you to stir up the gift of God which is in you through the laying on of my hands. For God has not given us a spirit of fear, but of power and of love and of a sound mind."
2 Timothy 1:5-7 (NKJV)

Graciously, God has gifted me my very own family, and I am beyond grateful for their lessons, too. I have learned what true unconditional love is from my husband José. He's seen me at my worst and still believed in my best. Not once have I felt that I had to perform, act, or be something different in order to merit his love. He's never let me feel like I could lose or lessen his love for me. Exemplifying God's love in its truest form, José shows me daily what Christ's love for His bride looks like as he sacrifices for me and our kids to have the best. Neither José nor I are perfect. We've had more than our fair share of struggles, but our willingness to pursue God's ideal is strong. We've both learned to go through the various stages and seasons of our lives together.

In my four children, I see hope. Hope for a tomorrow that is better than today. Hope that I have a chance to undo the wrongs done to me and do right by them. Hope that the legacy which started with my parents, grandparents, and great-grandparents will continue forward for generations to come.

Each of my children has a unique purpose, a special name given to them by God, and a story of their own.

Caitlyn-Alexis

My first child was born, August 14, 1999. Everything about her was perfect. Her face was beautiful without any tell-tale signs of recent delivery. Her cries were very feminine, and once she was placed in my arms, she was quiet and calm, as if she instantly knew she belonged there.

She was quick and intelligent right from the start and had a keen sense of judgment when it came to people she allowed herself to trust. She potty-trained herself by the time she was a year and a half, and by three years old, she already had the mental and verbal knowledge of a six-year-old.

Always thinking and wanting to *do* something, the thing that came naturally to her was cooking. When all her peers brought cookies made by their moms or purchased at a store, Caitlyn was baking and decorating entire cakes. Though she would never agree to enter a beauty contest or sing in front of our church, my little nine-year-old won at the sectional and district levels in the baking category for Missionettes competitions. She would say she wanted to be a professional chef, but the idea of actually being a *food critic* amused her. When I read her writing and the way she clearly and adequately relates her ideas, I wonder if there is not a writer in her as well.

Before we had kids, I thought it would be cute to give all our children "J" names to match José and me. After nine hours of labor, the idea of giving all our kids names that began with "J" slipped my mind. I had always liked the names Caitlyn and Alexis. They sounded pretty to me, and I loved that they meant "pure" and "helper and defender of mankind."

I gave my firstborn daughter this beautiful name, but later wondered if I had made a mistake. In service one Sunday, I remembered my "J" idea. I played around with the idea of legally changing Caitlyn's name until I felt the Lord tell my heart, *You did not name her. I did.*

From that point on, I've known God has special plans for my firstborn daughter. In her childhood, I awaited those plans anxiously as I watched her grow every day.

Caitlyn is very much like me – independent, knows what she wants, and yet puts herself second to go with the choices of her loved ones. She is quiet and shy at first, watching carefully for whom she can open her heart to; and once she does, she is loyal and faithful to the end. She loves to laugh, and you will often find her near someone who is acting silly.

I call her my *essence.* I understand her intensity coupled with her gentle heart and quiet spirit that, when in its element, soars high, strong, and majestically. It will be exciting to see where God uses this "helper and defender of mankind" that He named Himself, and the purpose behind why He did!

Karissa-Leiann

I surprised José on Father's Day of 2000 with the news that we were expecting our second child. Certain that this must be *the boy*, our baby shower consisted of yellow, green, and blue baby items.

On Super Bowl Sunday, January 28, 2001, our Karissa was born. Though she was red and purple with her face squished up, I could see that she was very beautiful. Her name came about when José dreamed he was chasing a little girl, running around and calling out, "Karissa! Leiann!"

She has always had stronger Velazquez features and, at a very young age, resembled her great-grandmother Mama Clarita. My sister-in-law Margarita spent that summer with us, and as she carried Karissa, people would ask if Karissa was *her* baby. As she grew up, Karissa had a hard time realizing that when people said she looked like her daddy, it was a *good* thing and not that they were telling her she looked like a boy.

Karissa's natural giftedness comes in the form of art, colors, and design. She finds beauty in everything flora and fauna, and is able to see *beyond* what normal eyes can behold.

She started speaking a little later in life and was cautious as she approached other milestones. When Karissa *did* decide to start talking, she spoke in long, complex sentences. To this day, she is very elaborate when describing or explaining something, an attribute that helps draw others into what she is trying to relay.

I would often hear her practicing what she wanted to tell me down the hall. I struggled to let her say what she needed to after I had heard the conversation just minutes before. When Karissa was required to practice her handwriting, her letters looked exactly like the samples on the page – angle for angle, curve for curve, dot for dot. She was only in second grade, and her penmanship was better than most people I knew.

Deliberate in everything she does, Karissa makes the world around her beautiful. When she was younger, it took her a little longer to make friends with kids her own age, but Karissa easily made friends with people older than her. She could effortlessly carry very intelligent conversations with any adult, and little ones always gravitated toward her.

I call her my *heart* because she is very sincere, tender-hearted, and has a passion for the world and everyone in it. She sees the good in all things and loves to dance. Wearing a mantle similar to mine, when I can't find the words, Karissa not only knows *what* I'm trying to say but *how* I would want to say it. Her name means "beloved" and "beauty and light," and she lives true to these names.

Growing up, she would say she wanted to be an artist and hang her paintings in a museum. When it came to planning the cover of *this* book, there was no doubt in my mind she would be the one to design it.

We went on a mission trip to Costa Rica when Karissa was three, and she came back saying she wanted to be a missionary. She loves babies and is always smiling at or holding the nearest baby to her. Karissa always wanted to buy the latest baby doll or animal at the toy store, and she told us she wanted to have four kids one day – twin boys and twin girls. A dreamer at heart, I encouraged her that all her gifts, talents, and things she loves are all put there by God. He already gives her visions, and she sees things most people are not even aware of in the spiritual realm. He is molding all these aspects of Karissa together to make her a vessel to be used by Him for His glory and honor.

Joscelyn-Analei

Our third daughter, Joscelyn, was a little harder to come by. The "plan" had been to get married, wait two years, then have four kids – one every two years – and be done by the time I turned thirty. That was the plan, but when we tried for our third, we found ourselves wondering if we could ever get pregnant again. We had become pregnant with Caitlyn and Karissa pretty easily, but I became worried when we tried to get pregnant a third time with no results.

I was relieved when a pregnancy test came back positive. But after a month passed, I lost the baby. I was completely crushed. So many questions entered my mind as to what I could have done wrong, whether I would ever conceive again, if something in my reproductive system was wrong . . . The endless questions put so much stress on me.

Months went by and nothing – no pregnancy. José was strong and faithful. He told me to be patient, take it easy, and leave it in God's hands.

But *my* plan was quickly slipping through my fingers like sand. The stronger I tried to grasp onto it, the more it slipped out. I persuaded José to take me to my doctor. She basically repeated everything he had told me – take it easy, relax, and, to my surprise, she even told me to leave it in God's hands. I prayed, thanked God for the two precious little girls I already had, acknowledged in my heart that He knew what was best for me, and I felt myself loosen that grip and leave it in His hands.

A few months later, during Christmas time, we found out we were expecting. We'd chosen to find out the gender of our *first* baby because we wanted to make sure we had everything we needed. With our second, we wanted it to be a surprise. We secretly believed it would be our boy, and then we had our *second* girl. With this next baby, we chose to find out the gender just in case this one was the boy. We learned we were having our *third* girl!

We were amazed and a little in disbelief at the odds of having *another* little girl. Worried we may not be able to have another child because we struggled to have this one, we named her Joscelyn Analei. Joscelyn has her dad's name; we inserted a "c" to avoid any mispronunciation by our Spanish-speaking family members who might interpret her name to be "little female José." We included "lyn" in the spelling of her name to honor her sister Caitlyn. Analei not only has Ann – my middle name – in it, but it is also Karissa's middle name switched around.

She was born on September 2, 2003. When I placed her in her crib, she would look up at me with such intensity from her huge eyes, and I swore my precious little baby girl actually saw straight into my soul.

Always laughing, smiling, and hugging everyone around her, I call Joscelyn my *spirit* as I see her watching and learning from those around her. She is able to learn and catch things simply by observing. At five years old, the thing that stood out the most was her desire to help with anything as long as she was near people and working. She works with all her heart and strength, never complaining about the task at hand. She simply enjoys doing something *with* and *for* someone. This isn't too surprising considering everyone who saw her immediately wanted to hold her and love her when she was just a few months old. *Everyone.*

One of our friends from church had miscarried, and while her husband and I were in choir practice, she would sit holding and loving Joscelyn. My little baby allowed herself to be used by God to bring healing to a hurting heart. True to her name which means "just" and "gracious," she loves to serve, is quick to learn, and seeks for there to be justice in the lives of all those around her. She won't find out until she reads this, but someone recently shared with me that they had a vision of me dancing around in a white dress. Dancing alongside me was Joscelyn in a similar white dress.

I look with excitement and anticipation to see all God will do through Joscelyn. Already, she is more than I ever was.

Joseph-Peter

During worship on a Wednesday night service, I had the greatest urge to go up to the altar to pray and sit in God's presence. That was an unusual thing to do on a Wednesday where the format was more like a study than a worship service. But the urge was strong. No one else was up there and at four months' pregnant with our fourth and last child, it was not exactly easy for me to hide. I looked around and thought I caught the eye of our worship leader, the pastor's wife, but then we both looked away. I thought, *If she sings one more song, that will be my sign to go up, because then I'll know I have time to pray at the altar before worship time is over.* But she did not.

We finished the song, went through the study of that evening, and then an odd thing happened: they did an altar call. Positive *that* was my sign, I got ready to go up when, all of a sudden, José walked up to pray. He *never* did that, and since I had Joscelyn sleeping in her car seat next to me, only one of us could go up. The church service ended and José was talking to the pastors at the front of the church. I walked up to say hello.

Our pastor's wife looked at me pensively, started to say something, and hesitated. I asked her what she wanted to tell me and she paused as her eyes began to well up with tears. She proceeded to tell me that the Lord told her something during worship. She had told the Lord, *If this is really from You, have Judy come up to the altar.* Since I never came up, she was hesitant to tell me in case she was wrong.

I told her what I had been experiencing at my seat during worship and it was a confirmation for her.

"The Lord showed me that your son is going to be a prophet."

I gasped! I floundered between being excited that after three girls we were going to have a *son* and surprised the Lord would use my son in such a way. Both great news! We began to cry and hug.

The pastor's wife and I kept God's message between us until the night of our staff Christmas dinner, the same evening of our ultrasound where we found out that we were, indeed, going to have a son.

Choosing a name was both important and somewhat easy for this little man of ours who would be completing the count of Velazquez kids. Joseph-Peter carries the name of his father *and* his grandfather, the two most important men in my life. Joseph means "He shall add" and Peter means "rock."

On May 5, 2005, this son of ours added to the joy and amusement of our family. He is always animated with surprisingly accurate facts about Greek mythology, science, and the Bible. Retaining anything he reads or hears, there's no doubt that God is filling his mind and heart in preparation for all the things this boy will do in the world, reflecting and projecting God's love. Joseph's dad is his biggest hero, he tells me I look beautiful all the time, and he simply adores each of his sisters. They hold a specific place of honor in his heart.

Joseph is not just a part of me; as with his sisters, he is an extension of me, my *sonshine*. We speak with a language all our own, have lofty dreams about the future, and can be feisty at times and tender-hearted at others. I had always wanted a brother so that somehow my dad's legacy would live on. God knew better and gave me a son – a son who was born two years before my dad passed away.

When Joseph was five years old, he asked me to pray for him.

"Mommy can you pray for God to guide my hands and teach me to play piano?"

I cried. By the time *this* Peter was a teen, not only had he learned piano easily, but he had also composed some of his own original songs – just like his Grandpa Peter.

In their youth, I saw my kids *already* being used in powerful ways by God, and as they now approach adulthood I can honestly say I'm excited for what's next. I started life feeling so lonely, and I am so grateful to God for blessing me with my very own family.

"My son, do not forget my teaching, but keep my commands in your heart, for they will prolong your life many years and bring you peace. Let love and faithfulness never leave you; bind them around your neck, write them on the tablet of your heart. Then you will win favor and a good name in the sight of God and man. Trust in the Lord with all your heart and lean not on your own understanding; in all your ways submit to Him, and He will make your paths straight."
Proverbs 3:1-6 (NIV)

Chapter Eleven

HELD

"With passion I pursue and cling to you. Because I feel your
grip on my life, I keep my soul close to your heart."
Psalms 63:8 (TPT)

I had asked God three things throughout my life:
When will You heal my dad?

Why did You let my dad get sick?

And . . .

If You choose not to heal him, could you please let my dad speak to me
before he dies?

Two of those three things had been answered. The first was answered in my teen years: whenever He wanted, He would. God had promised that *He* would be my dad. And if He *did* heal my dad, it would come only in the manner in which it would draw others to Him and bring Him the glory. That night, I hadn't received a *yes* or a *no,* but rather a *wait* and a promise from God that He would be my Abba Father. Most likely, He would not heal my dad, but there was always the knowledge that if He wanted to, He could. I was determined to hold onto that hope until I heard otherwise.

My second question was answered when I was twenty-seven. Why did God let my dad get sick? God answered, *Because he was willing.*

God's love for us is unfathomable, and those who truly understand the magnitude of His love for themselves and the world are the ones desiring to love Him back with their lives, to reach the lost no matter the cost.

On January 4, 2007, the year I was to turn thirty-two, God answered my third and final request. José and I were in bed at 11:00 p.m. when the phone rang. No one called that late except for Mom, and she usually only let it ring twice. If I didn't answer by the second ring and it wasn't important, she would figure I must be busy or asleep and hang up without leaving a message.

On this night, the phone rang once, twice, three times, and then the answering machine picked up. I sat up to listen to the recording from the machine downstairs in the kitchen.

Throughout my married life, a late-night phone call with a message meant Mom was on the way to the hospital with Dad because something was wrong. The "somethings" had become increasingly more vital since 1999, when Dad got pseudomonas. The late-night calls were becoming more serious than a high fever or bad cold from my childhood days when Dad's illnesses weren't as severe. I waited to hear what her message said, knowing I was most likely going to get up to meet her at the hospital depending how serious things were.

I couldn't possibly have ever been prepared for *this* message.

"Judy? *Judy*! Judy, wake up. I *need* you!"

She didn't yell, yet her tone told me something was *really* wrong.

Not just the tone that my dad was really sick. Not just the tone that my dad was really, *really* sick. This was *so* different from anything I'd ever heard from Mom before.

I jumped out of bed, grabbed clothes to change into, and ran downstairs to pick up the phone. I called her while scrambling to get dressed at the same time.

"What happened?!"

"You need to come."

"I'll be right there!" I understood without being told.

José asked if I wanted him to go instead and I told him no. I could *not* risk Dad passing away without me by his side. Besides, I had asked God to let Dad speak to me before he died. *I have to be there.*

I drove to Mom's house praying and pleading and speaking in tongues the whole way. "Please God, don't let him die without me getting to say goodbye. Please, please, *please* God. I *have* to see him before he dies. *Please!*"

I repeated this all nine and a half minutes of my drive. There were green lights the whole way. It was late at night and no one else was on the streets which was likely a factor, but I also believe God let all the lights turn green, *for me.*

I ran inside the house to my dad's room. He was pale and cold. Mom was leaning over my dad in his hospital bed gently stroking his head and cheek.

"It's your daddy's time to go. You need to say goodbye."

What? I stared at her in disbelief knowing there was absolutely nothing I could do to slow down time, to make what was happening – however ready I was or not – just stop.

I looked into his eyes. They were glazed over. It was, no doubt, his time to go.

My heart was crushed that I might have missed his passing. I whimpered. Without any words, my spirit reached God before my mind or heart could.

And then, I saw a twinkle. Oh, so faint, but I *saw* it!

I *know* in my heart that it was not my imagination, and I *know* that regardless of the situation, whether my dad had passed before I got there or not, I know that in His infinite mercy, God allowed my dad one last glimpse at me and I of him before passing to be with the Lord. That glimpse was mine to keep forever. The Lord allowed me to *see* my dad before he left completely. The same way I would notice Joscelyn as an infant looking deep into my soul, I caught that same look in Dad's eyes as our souls connected in a split second. And then he was gone.

I told Dad I loved him, whispered in his ear that he was my silent hero for those thirty-two years, thanked him for all he had done for us – known and unknown – and kissed his cheek one last time.

I called José and asked him to bring our kids so they could say goodbye to their grandpa.

The day of Dad's burial, I sat there knowing it was *all* gone. *All of it.* No hope of God healing my dad, no hope of my dad speaking words to me before passing. *Nothing.*

I had *nothing* and sat there accepting, once again, that God did as He chose. Whether or not I understood what He did, I knew He loved me. I knew everything He did was just and right and fair and *always* in love. I knew not to complain, so I numbly accepted it all.

There's a difference between joyfully accepting what God does in our life and numbly accepting it. I may have been numb because of my mind's own defense mechanism to the stress that followed the night I lost my dad until his burial, but regardless of the cause of my numbness, I had given up.

Hope, *gone.*

The picture of me standing by my dad that night in the Angeles Temple – brave, strong, and hopeful – tormented my mind. My heart was troubled for that little girl who believed so much, endured so much, and, in the end, didn't get anything.

In the quiet at the end of the burial service, as we waited for the tractor to bring dirt to cover Dad's coffin, I mourned for that little girl. Where was she? I couldn't feel her. She was gone deep in my heart somewhere, too devastated to join me in mourning. Too far gone to join me in the healing. I couldn't reach her and, in my own numbness, I let her stay away.

"Would anyone like to say anything?" My Tío Luis broke the silence. No one did.

I felt awful because I didn't have anything to say, and neither did anyone else. No one had anything to say about my dad as a person except for those who knew him before he had gotten sick, and they couldn't say anything out of grief.

Finally, Tía Gladys walked forward. What a relief. It was just like her to ease an uncomfortable situation. On behalf of my dad's side of the family, she offered kind words to my mom for taking such good care of Dad for thirty-two years.

Then she turned to me, looked me in the eyes, and said, "Judy, if your dad could speak to you, He would want you to know . . ." and Tía Gladys began to share the words my heart longed to hear that my mind would have never been able to articulate on its own: My dad loved me. My dad would be so proud of the woman I had become, would love José like his own son, and would simply adore the four grandkids I had given him. He would want me to know that he knew I had been brave through it all and that, even in my failures, my tenacity to hang on to God no matter what was the very desire of my dad's heart. My dad would want me to know that he would miss me for a little while but would meet me one day up in Heaven. *That* was God's promise and recompense for these past thirty-two years.

I sat there in awe of God's mercy toward an undeserving child who didn't merit a single thing in life. I had already been given the ultimate gift of having His son, Jesus Christ, die on the cross for the redemption of *my* sins. Eternal life was already more than I ever deserved; and yet, in thirty-two years, I had also experienced God as my Abba Father in ways many people will never experience Him.

In humble gratitude, I understood in my spirit that God was giving me my last request to hear my dad speak. Not in the form I had asked or imagined. Not through the very lips of my own father, but through the lips of Dad's sister who had been a constant source of identity for my dad's side of the family, the other half of me, the link between my present and my past.

In her sincere obedience to the Lord, Tía Gladys allowed herself to be used by God to be my own dad's voice, *audible*. My very desire, answered. *God's way.* His perfect way. Her words would be the healing balm to my mind's torment, my heart's devastation, my soul's lament, and yet my spirit's recompense!

I would like to say that I was a fortitude of strength and hope, that I was full of joy that my dad no longer suffered in his earthly body, that I would miss him, but knew he was free in Heaven. I wish I could say I was sad, but could look in anticipation of the day we would be reunited and I would get to meet Dad for the very first time . . . I was not. I was *lost*. I couldn't grasp what was happening. *How can it all be over?* There were no warnings, no signs of an illness that would cost him his life, and it all was a tornado of confusion. Throughout those thirty-two years, Dad had been so healthy that doctors said he could live well into his eighties.

I kneeled down on the cold earth beside his casket, longing for one last *something* before his body was lowered into the ground, never to be seen again. I lost it.

Gone. He was just *gone*. My story. My life. All of it, just *gone*.

Someone lifted me from the ground, and I placed my white rose on top of Dad's casket. I took one last glance over my shoulder as I heard chains rattling in preparation for the casket's descent. I can't remember if I was there as they lowered the casket or not. I know I would have *wanted* to watch until the last mound of dirt was placed over it, but I went numb and I have no memory.

Natalie Grant has a poignant song entitled "Held." These are a few of the lyrics:

> Who told us we'd be rescued?
> What has changed and why should we
> be saved from nightmares?
> We're asking why this happens
> To us who have died to live?
> It's unfair.
>
> This is what it means to be held.
> How it feels when the sacred
> is torn from your life
> And you survive.
> This is what it is to be loved.
> And to know that the promise was
> When everything fell, we'd be held.
>
> This hand is bitterness.
> We want to taste it, let the

hatred numb our sorrow.
The wise hand opens slowly to
lilies of the valley and tomorrow.

If hope is born of suffering,
If this is only the beginning,
Can we not wait for one hour
watching for our Savior?

This is what it means to be held.
How it feels when the sacred
is torn from your life
And you survive.

This is what it is to be loved.
And to know that the promise was
When everything fell, we'd be held.

As I walked away from Dad's burial site, I felt it. I just knew as it started happening that I felt *it*. Through the numbness. Through the pain. *It* was there. Slowly, tightly, securely. And with glints of the familiar Divine Love I had felt throughout the years – nearly imperceptible, yet unmistakably there – my *spirit* bore witness to it all once again. God's love was wrapping itself around me, whether I wanted it to or not. God's love was weaving in, around, and through me. Around my body. Around my mind. Around my soul. Around my heart.

I numbly surrendered to it.

I entered the chrysalis once more . . . already feeling the oozing feeling of becoming liquified into the nothingness for the process of "transformation." I was aware I was *held*. Even if all of me but my spirit was destroyed, I knew I was held. *Abba* held me. And I welcomed being hidden as the pain of being *seen* was much too unbearable.

> *"When you did awesome things that we did not look for,*
> *you came down, the mountains quaked at your presence.*
> *From of old no one has heard*
> *or perceived by the ear,*
> *no eye has seen a God besides you,*
> **who acts for those who wait for him.**
> *You meet him who joyfully works righteousness,*
> *those who remember you in your ways.*
> *Behold, you were angry, and we sinned;*
> *in our sins we have been a long time, and shall we be saved?*
> *But now, O Lord, you are our Father;*
> *we are the clay, and you are our potter;*
> **we are all the work of your hand.**"
>
> Isaiah 64:3-5, 8, emphasis mine

Chapter Twelve

IF I BE LIFTED UP

"And I, when I am lifted up from the earth,
will draw all people to Myself."
John 12:32

Both of my parents were musicians, but, somehow, the talent skipped me. I can hold a note, but I can't *truly* sing, and those years of piano lessons did not pay off. *At all.* Regardless, music remains within me and has always been a great part of my life, especially the songs that seemed to play during the most pivotal seasons of my life.

Perhaps it was because I lived vicariously through the Von Trapp family from *The Sound of Music*, which played over and over in my house from childhood until this day. I watched the seven kids learn the do-re-mi's and how to run to the hills to twirl and sing from the beautiful Fraulein Maria. I learned your problems could be fixed by singing about a few of your favorite things and, when you did, you didn't feel so bad.

I also took away from musicals that "somewhere over the rainbow" life was in technicolor, the way it was *supposed* to be where you realize all you ever needed was resolved in the simple fact that "there's no place like home."

Watching *Annie* oddly made Dad being sick so much more bearable. Knowing a little orphan girl, surrounded by horrible people, could be loved and change the world around her, moved me. Annie's longing for love from unknown parents, defending herself against bullies, and hope that "the sun will come out tomorrow" made the tomorrows of my own life something I *could* believe in.

There are two songs that played constantly in the days of my childhood. It was as if they had been written while my early life was unfolding, somehow knowing what Mom and I were going through.

"You and Me Against the World," by Helen Reddy was our anthem. It was just the two of us against all odds, against what the cultural norm stated we should be and how we should act. As a young, hispanic, single mom with a "fatherless" daughter, we *should* have faced insurmountable issues; and yet, there we were, tearing society's standards down as our relationship with God proved us capable of rising up above it all. We felt God faithfully lift us up above the storm time after time.

Although Mom would sing "Best Thing That Ever Happened to Me," by Gladys Knight & the Pips in reference to *me*, the song definitely could've been written from me to *her*. I can't imagine if I would have had a mother who *did* choose to leave her sick husband behind without giving me the chance to have a tangible relationship with my dad, however limited that was. What if she hadn't taught me to be strong in the Lord and to trust in Him at all times? What if she hadn't chosen to fight with the Lord by her side?

Mom has always been strong in my eyes. Rita Lopez was the fifth child of seven, born to migrant workers who followed the seasonal crops along Southern and Central California. Working in the fields by the age of five between her two brothers taught her to be strong and have an outstanding work ethic. As one of five girls, Mom learned to stand on her own while still seeing the beauty in others. Growing up in God's plan caused her to love Him as few others would ever come to realize.

Living strong and loving even stronger, Mom always found strength and joy in the Lord. She leaned heavily on Him for His divine grace, mercy, and guidance as she walked the path prepared for her. God would be her husband, and, as she walked with Him, she held her head high with unwavering faith. There were times when things were extremely difficult – sometimes downright unbearable – but God's continual reminders sustained her over and over again.

Mom was, and is, consistently a living testimony of God's greatness in the lives of those who trust Him at all times and for all things. By her own example of trusting God to lift her up, to lift *us* up above our situation, I have been able to weather extremely difficult times throughout my own life. *She* is the "best thing that ever happened to *me*" as Gladys Knight sings.

If you were to mention a specific time in my life, I could tell you where God met me and what song was ministering to me in that season. Like a real-life musical, there are songs that have played so purposefully in the soundtrack of my life. Songs that speak to my entire being, bringing me to my knees in praise to God for all He is, has done, and will do.

It isn't any surprise that a new soundtrack began to play weeks after Dad's funeral. Weeks after staying at Mom's house so she wouldn't be alone, weeks after being brave, of holding it all together so everyone else could see that I was okay. Weeks of *yet again* fighting against cultural norms that told me I should be mad at God and rage against Him for the "evil" He had bestowed upon Mom and me for thirty-two years.

I returned to our own home with José and the kids, exhausted and still very numb to the surreal life I had lived and the ordeals of those past weeks. New to the feelings of sheer vastness of what the rest of my life would look like now that *for sure* God was never going to heal my dad, I walked upstairs to my room.

"I just need some time to myself." I feigned that I was okay as best I could.

I didn't know it until later, but my little family of five prayed and battled and warred downstairs on my behalf. A legacy of strength in God continued from my ancestors to my own children.

Quietly, I closed the door to our bedroom, turned on our local Christian radio station to drown out the sound, and collapsed onto the floor in a pile of misery, grief, and shock. I allowed my heart and mind to imagine myself crawling up into my Abba Father's lap, placing my head on His chest. I waited for that familiar feeling of His arms wrapping around me, and I cried as I had never cried before.

Just like that, the perfect soundtrack for the moment began to play on the radio – "Came To My Rescue" by Hillsong:

Falling on my knees in worship
Giving all I am to seek Your face
Lord, all I am is Yours

My whole life I place in Your hands
God of Mercy humbled I bow down
In Your presence at Your throne

I called, You answered
And You came to my rescue
And I wanna be where You are ...

In my life be lifted high
In our world be lifted high
In our love be lifted high

Nearly immediately after the coroner had removed Dad's body on the night he passed away, Mom shut the door to his room, keeping the entire world out – even those of us there in the house – and she worshiped God.

I *heard* her. She worshiped and cried and praised and spoke in tongues and lamented and groaned. Then, she worshiped some more. It was the most *powerful* thing I had ever heard, the most tender, empowering thing in my entire life. Dad's death was tearing Mom apart; yet, as she worshiped, I heard the Lord mercifully put her back together again.

So when *I* got home, I closed my door. I shut out the entire world, worshiped, and met God in my room. More importantly, He met *me.*

Throughout Dad's illness, I saw glimpses of the valley of the shadow of death: watching him experience seizures, his G-tube falling out and the stomach acid burning his flesh, calling 911 in sixth grade while dispatch questioned whether I truly knew what spinal meningitis was, and the disbelief in her voice that my dad had been in a coma for so long. For months during junior high, I did homework in Dad's hospital room to advocate for him if nurses or doctors tried to do anything I felt was questionable without Mom's consent. I was close to death, and yet God was closer.

> *"There were no warriors in Israel until I, Deborah,*
> *arose, until I arose to be a mother to Israel."*
> Judges 5:7 (NCV)

I had spent thirty-two years completely aware that everything I was, was because of God and the example *both* my parents had shown me in their own distinct way. Mom was a Bible character lived out in-person for me to learn from. In God's Word, the Prophet Deborah stood alongside a man who was unable – and unwilling – to fight without her. Deborah willingly engaged in a battle that was not originally hers.

Similarly, as God took Mom down paths which ran against cultural norms, she knew God alone would help her obtain victory. Mom has the wisdom and strength of Deborah, the beauty and grace of Esther "for such a time as this," the hard work and stamina of Martha, and the waiting and listening heart of Mary. By any means, she uses all her gifts and talents for God. There are many great women in this world and in God's Word, but none compare to my mom.

That little girl who picked strawberries at the age of five, wore hand-me-downs from three older sisters, and struggled to complete the school year's end because her family had to travel for work . . .

That teenager who committed her life to God and His Word, who obeyed the call to go to the Bible institute . . .

That young bride who, at the age of twenty-four, held the life, or *death*, of her husband in her hands and dedicated her life to care for him at home with her daughter . . .

The beautiful and strong pastor, grandmother to my children, and friend to my heart . . .

That woman is my hero and she is my *mom*. I am who I am today because of who she is, who she *had to be*.

Through the emptying of *both* my parents' lives, I learned to trust God. Whether He chose to take their life or mine, I knew in His face alone was love, peace, mercy, and grace.

The night God promised to be my dad, I gave my all to Him in complete surrender. Everything in my life was His to do as He best saw fit. I walked in complete faith that God is love, and from the abundance of His love, my pain could be entrusted to Him. From within the whirlwind of love and pain, there could, indeed, be a resolve of praise.

Truly, there was no other choice for me than to place my whole life in God's hands. He had proven to me, time after time, that in His hands was where I needed to remain if I were to survive and thrive. In His hands was the safest place for me to be. There were times when His hands would be open for me to see the world and have the world see me, and others when He would close His hands over me in protection against things on the outside attempting to take me out.

I'm humbled that God would even look at me, much less use me or interact with me. And He continues to do so. My response is to bow before Him, not in humiliation, but in sheer adoration. Submission to Him is not the relinquishing of who I am, but the acknowledgement that He desires for me to be so much more than I currently am.

God lifts us out of our desperate situations so that we can then lift *Him* up for others to see His saving grace and, in turn, be saved.

> *"And I, when **I am lifted up** from the earth,*
> *will draw all people to Myself."*
> John 12:32 (NIV, emphasis mine)

My parents, Rita and Peter, on their wedding day on June 9, 1973

My parents, pregnant with me in 1975.

Mom, me, and Dad in April, 1975. I was three weeks old.

Dad and me when I was two and a half months old.

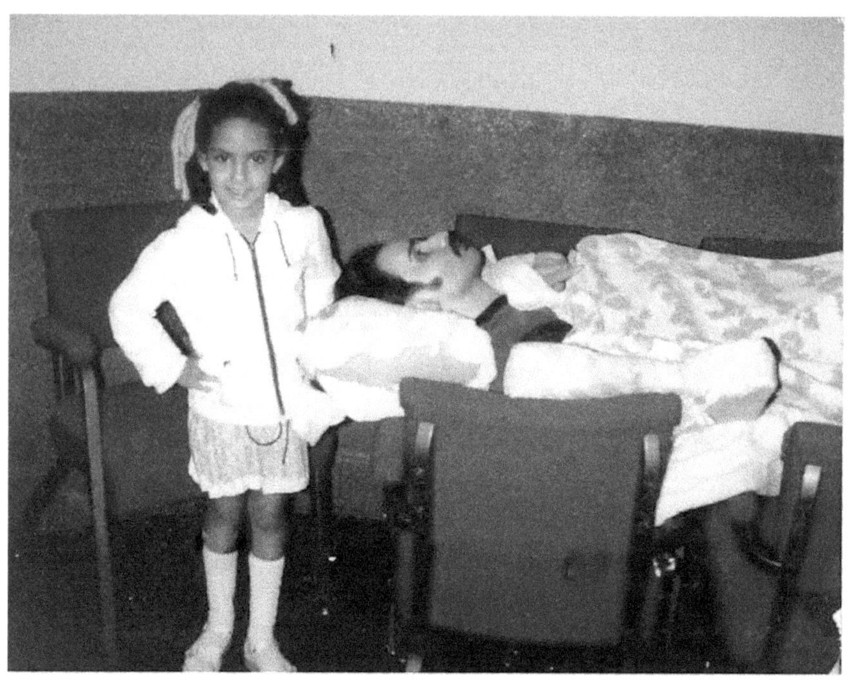

Me and Dad at the prayer service at Angeles Temple in October, 1980.

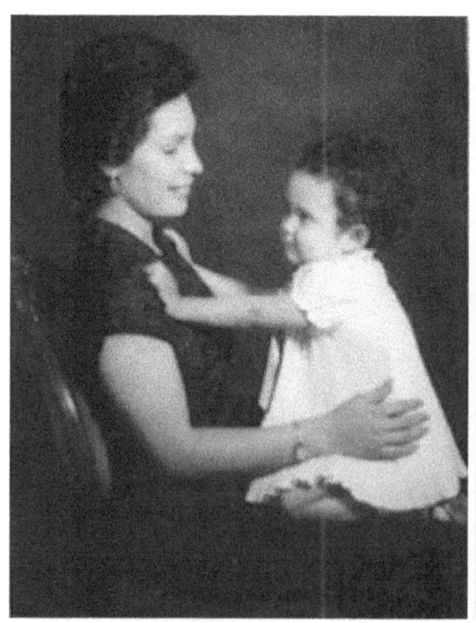

Mom and me, 1976.

Me on my quinceañera with Mom, 1990.

LABI College, 1993. I'm in the center front, and José is directly above me in the back row.

LABI College Board of Trustees. I served from 2015-2021.

Me at Missionettes Camp in June, 1989.

Preaching at Girls Ministries Camp (formerly Missionettes Camp) in July, 2019.

The Lopez Family
Back row: Rosie, Tina, Tony, Linda, Martha, Rita (Mom)
Front row: Basil Jr., Rosario (Rosie), Basilio (Basil)

The Perez Family
Back row: Judy, Rita, Carlos Sr., Peter Sr., Gladys, Rick, Olvido, Barbara, Ruben
Front row: Julianka, Naomi, Lucinda, Jasmine, Leticia, Jeremy, Israel, Carlos Jr.

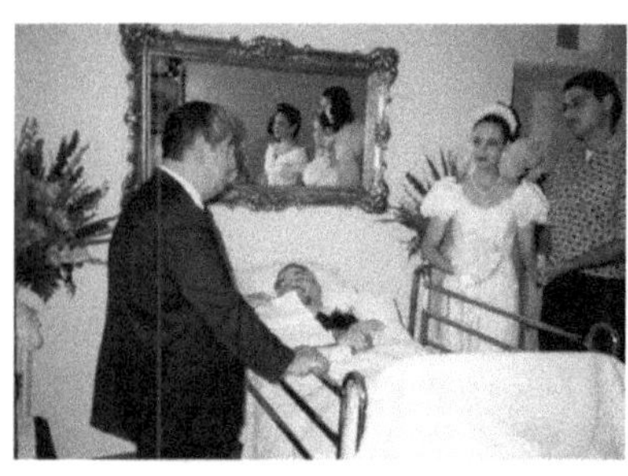

*Our wedding ceremony with
Dad on May 24, 1997.*

Mom walking me down the aisle.

Our wedding at Grand Tradition on May 24, 1997.

The Velazquez Six:
José, me, Caitlyn, Karissa, Joscelyn, and Joseph

May, 2006.

November, 2009.

February, 2019.

Launching CityWide Mosaic in Temecula on January 12, 2020.

Our twenty-fifth anniversary in May, 2022.
From left: Joscelyn, Caitlyn, me, José, Karissa, and Joseph

Caitlyn & Sal's wedding in December, 2020.
From left: Joseph, José, Joscelyn, me, Karissa, Caitlyn, and Sal

Family vacation to Hawaii in August, 2021.

IMAGO STAGE

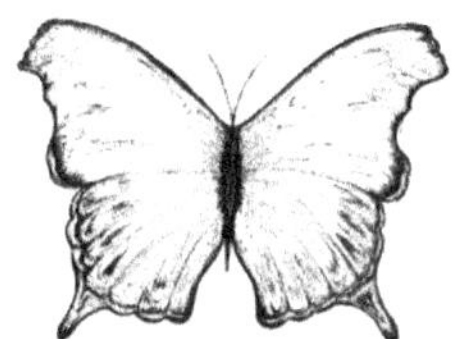

The day before a butterfly emerges, enzymes weaken the chrysalis, making it fragile and brittle. Its wings are softer than silk at this moment and still very small. Its fat body is filled with fluid which is then pumped into very thin veins in its wings. In just ten minutes, the wings are full size. They are still very soft and need two to three hours to harden. Then, the wings flop out of the chrysalis, followed by the butterfly's body in a matter of seconds. This is the only time a butterfly grows, and it's all over within fifteen minutes. The emergence of the butterfly is called *eclosion*.

In biology, the *imago,* or "image," is the last stage an insect attains during its metamorphosis – process of growth and development. It is also called the imaginal stage, the stage in which the insect attains maturity.

"A monarch butterfly lives as a chrysalis for two weeks. A swallowtail butterfly may choose to stay as a chrysalis for over a year. While both are butterflies, each undergoes a uniquely-timed metamorphic phase that contributes to its success in becoming fully themselves. Your chrysalis is incomparable to the chrysalis of those around you. While we're all made of the same substance that makes us genuinely human, we're all transforming into something uniquely, yet familiarly, beautiful. And all in a timing perfectly catered to who we're meant to become."

~ Caitlyn Alexis

Chapter Thirteen

DELIGHT YOURSELF IN THE LORD

"Delight yourself in the LORD, and He will give
you the desires of your heart."
Psalms 37:4

It was Christmas Eve, 2008, and we were home from church. We had taken the mattresses off of our beds and put them out in the living room. We planned to stay up until midnight on Christmas morning so the kids could open their presents. José lit a fire in the fireplace and we turned on the Christmas tree lights. We'd rented eight Christmas movies to watch during our long holiday break, and, with homemade goodies in hand, we prepared ourselves to watch movies until it was time to open presents.

Something was different this year. We had survived all the "firsts" that came throughout our first year without Dad. We had purchased a new home closer to José's work where we could start building equity of our own. Thanksgiving had breezed by. The holiday season had passed quickly. I didn't feel the stress of cooking like I had years before. I'd kept to my traditions, but, this year it hadn't been important to me to make the entire Thanksgiving meal from scratch, and, instead of the usual eight homemade desserts, I only made five. It was not "perfect," yet it was.

The days following Thanksgiving had whizzed by as I prepared for our women's Christmas celebration. Once again, I felt no stress. A level of adrenaline was present as I prepared for the event, but I was working with such an awesome team of ladies, I didn't feel overwhelmed.

My two older girls, Caitlyn and Karissa, were participating in our church's float at the local parade. Because I was working on everything else, I put off preparing Karissa's Hawaiian outfit until the last minute. I struggled with the concept. How does a seven-year-old girl dress Hawaiian in the middle of winter, at night, in the freezing cold, on a float that travels a little over two miles per hour?

I knew it would be too long of a night for her to wear traditional garb. I opted for a wrap-around Hawaiian print fabric a friend had loaned me along with thermals, sweats, and five shirts underneath. I overdid it with the lei's, figuring the more the better to keep her throat and chest warm. With the same idea in mind, I added a bunch of flowers to her head too. Caitlyn was just as bundled up, but her costume from Spain hid the layers upon layers that she wore.

Once again, I was stress-free as my girls got dressed, we got the float going, and we sat waving and cheering for our church. I had no desire to go back to the sanctuary and set things up for the next day. Our women's event was wonderful, and we stayed in town for the evening's service.

The girls were old enough to know the value of money, so I gave them each thirty dollars to spend on Christmas presents for their siblings. It was so much fun watching them. A few times, the element of surprise needed to be reestablished when one would ask the other, "Is this what you would like for Christmas?"

I made sure my daughters bought something their siblings didn't already know they were going to get.

So there we were, bundled around our beautiful Christmas tree with plans to watch movies all night and open presents at 12:01 a.m. on Christmas morning. But by 11:45 p.m., almost everyone was asleep. I tucked Joseph, who was three years old, into his bed and told him to close his eyes. Within minutes, he was asleep. Caitlyn and I looked at each other – the only two awake.

"Should we wake everyone up?" she asked.

I told her it would probably be more enjoyable for everyone if we slept through the night and opened presents in the morning. Never too tired for a celebration, she wasn't exactly happy to postpone the festivities, but quickly understood and realized she was tired as well.

I grabbed her – my nine-year-old firstborn child – and retold the story she'd heard many times before of how her daddy and I announced we were expecting our first baby ten years earlier. On Christmas Eve, 1998, I decorated a small bag with iron-on baby decals and puffy paint that said, "Rain or shine, I'll stay at Grandma's anytime!" I filled it with travel-sized baby items and wrapped it up for Christmas.

During our annual family get-together with Mom's side of the family, we all handed out presents. Mom received my unmarked box. Per tradition in our family, we opened presents from youngest to oldest. I side-eyed the present on Mom's lap, knowing she would get the biggest surprise of her life.

As she opened her gift, she asked who it was from. No one said anything because no one knew who had given it to her. She read the outside, looked at the contents on the inside, and looked around with a smile as she tried to determine the giver of the strange gift. My cousin

Marina was immediately questioned because she had the youngest of the great-grandchildren, but she confessed it was not from her.

After some time of awkwardness, I bursted out, "It's from me!"

Everyone turned and looked at me with blank stares.

I said it again. "I'm pregnant!"

The group giggled, assuming I was joking. José and I had only been married a year and a half so no one imagined it was true. Not exactly the response I had wanted. Being pregnant and hormonal, I started to cry.

Finally, Marina shouted out, "You guys, I think she's serious! Are you pregnant, Judy?"

I stood up in the middle of the living room on top of all the wrapping paper mess and said, "Yes, I'm not kidding. I really *am* pregnant! I'm going to have a baby!"

Mom looked shocked, Nana looked confused, and my cousins and aunts came running up to me, hugging me and crying. Mom jumped up and gave me a big hug and kiss and told me how proud she was of me.

"This is the best Christmas present ever!" she told me.

Still confused, Nana asked her what was going on. Mom told her again in Spanglish, the household language of our fifth-generation family.

"Mamá, Judy va a tener un *baby*!"

Nana started crying and hugged me. Knowing José and I were officially starting our family was the best Christmas gift.

Ten years later, I found myself holding my firstborn little girl, enjoying the feeling that life was balancing out after the horrible previous year I had experienced. I was finally seeing the light coming out of the chrysalis I had been in.

Caitlyn lay down on her spot on the living room floor and fell asleep. I got up, made sure all the doors of our house were locked, and began to turn off the lights that had been left on. As I did, I looked around at our little house we had purchased only six months earlier. It was just the right size, had a pool, and we had decorated and landscaped the way we had always wanted. I turned off all the lights except for the Christmas tree and paused in the middle of my home to take it all in.

All of a sudden, it hit me! When I was little, we couldn't have a real Christmas tree because it would be dangerous for Dad if it caught on fire and we weren't home. That also meant no lit fireplace. As a child with an affinity for Christmas movies which included family traditions I was not privy to, I would take my blanket and pillow, place it under the fake Christmas tree sprayed with pine-smelling spray, and fall asleep mesmerized by the lights of the tree. Alone.

But this Christmas was different. I stood there as Holy Spirit opened my eyes to the crackling fireplace, our *real* Christmas tree, and the family I had wanted growing up. The family I had dreamed of – with the daddy, mommy, and kids all celebrating together – was now my very own. My dreams, my desires, had not been forgotten throughout my life. My Abba Father knew. He *remembered*. I hadn't been forgotten or forsaken. A price I thought I had paid by "accepting" my situation in life was being returned to me *above and beyond* what I had ever hoped for in the family I now had.

"O our God, we thank you and praise Your glorious name! But who am I, and who are my people, that we could give anything to You? **Everything we have has come from You**, *and we give You only what You first gave us!"*
1 Chronicles 29:13-14 (NLT, emphasis mine)

Throughout my life, I have always seen God give me favor with those around me. I liked to think that, as my Abba Father, He always gave me the best. When I look at my family, I know beyond a shadow of a doubt that God has given me the best. I *know* it. I feel it!

Everything my heart had ever desired throughout my life was fulfilled in that one moment on Christmas Eve. God, my Abba Father, continued to keep His promise to provide for me as a father would, including this little family of mine, *The Velazquez Six*!

"Delight yourself in the Lord, and He will give you the desires of your heart. Commit your ways to the Lord; trust in Him, and He will act. He will bring forth your righteousness as the light, and your justice as the noonday."
Psalm 37:4-6

Chapter Fourteen

IN HIS CHRYSALIS

"Therefore, if anyone is in Christ, he is a new creation.
The old has passed away; behold, the new has come."
2 Corinthians 5:17

Although God had told me to go into ministry as a child and I had dedicated my young adult years to studying at LABI College, my adult ministry "career" took many unexpected twists and turns.

In 2001, the Lord called José and me to a time of rest as He placed us in a chrysalis. We had been married for four years and had just brought our second daughter, Karissa, into the world. After God called us to leave our positions in Fallbrook, we found ourselves being refreshed at a church in Temecula. It was a time when we could just go to receive, rest, raise our family, and search God for our next steps.

It's interesting knowing God has placed a calling of ministry on your life and yet needing to rest. To the ears, it sounds like an oxymoron. To the eyes, it looks unimaginable. To the mind, it seems confusing. To the heart, it can be worrisome. But to the soul, it feels like the green pastures David writes about in Psalm 23.

We were so exhausted and burnt out that we regularly arrived at church late (*gasp!*) and left during the closing prayer. When asked to join small groups and various church events, we would decline. We were even asked once if we would like to accept Jesus Christ as our Lord and Savior!

More often than not, I found myself signing up for a women's event out of obligation, paying for it, and then deciding not to attend at the last minute. I didn't dare ask for a refund! I was too embarrassed, and that would mean more conversations and potentially hearing about the next event I would want to avoid.

Caitlyn did *not* like going into the nursery and actually enjoyed the adult service at three years old. She'd even laugh at the pastor's jokes. Karissa didn't mind going into the nursery, and I eventually succumbed to the obligatory rotation of helping in there every eight to ten weeks.

We were happy with the season we were in. The rest. The quiet. Walking in without any obligations and then walking right out. Our little family was happy and content just the way things were.

The thing about being called into ministry is that it's a calling deep within you. It's hard to escape because it's part of who you *are* as much as it is what you *do*. After a few months, I began to squirm about not serving in the church. A position opened up for a children's pastor, but God said no. A need for teachers came up, but again, no. I joined the worship team, but then changes were made and I got another no. Any leadership position always resulted in a no.

I started feeling lonely and needed women friends. A lady from church invited me to check out the latest kitchen gadgets, and I forced myself to go without knowing anyone. We were on a single income at home with two babies in diapers, so I took ten dollars and planned to purchase what I could for that amount. I was there to meet people and make friends, not shop. It worked! I slowly began to make more and more friends, many of whom I still have today.

In 2002, the Lord woke me up with the words "Philippians 3:9." Not the actual verse, just the text of where it was found. *Ministry* for me had been praying for the ladies at church and encouraging them in our friendships or with letters. Sometimes, I would stand at the back of the church and the Lord would reveal to me who I should pray for and what I should say. That night, when the Lord spoke the Bible reference, I got up and looked up what it said: "And be found in Him, not having a righteousness of my own that comes from the law, but that which is through faith in Christ – the righteousness that comes from God on the basis of faith."

I prayed and asked God who the verse was for so that I could pray for them. The message wasn't clear, so I read the verse in its context and was blown away by the revelation Holy Spirit showed me.

Throughout my life, I had depended on being good and always doing the right thing. I felt dependent on the fact that I never had any vices and that I never walked away from God at any point in my life. I was focused on what I was *doing* that made me right with God rather than the pure fact that my righteousness came solely through Jesus. Everything I had ever done, learned, and become was truly nothing compared to what Jesus had done, taught, and created in *me*. It didn't matter that *I* knew Jesus. What mattered was that *He* knew me.

I knew all this, but I didn't understand until that night. All the zeal I had for God that affected how I felt toward others who should know better – the heart of a Pharisee that I carried – was completely demolished that night as I realized my actions weren't better than anyone else because they were "right." My being right in Jesus was *despite* my right actions, which, in a sense were wrong because I had become dependent on them and even judgmental because of them.

That night, I learned to give grace to others and appreciate their journeys as long as they journeyed with God. I learned to give *myself* grace because I held a standard for myself that was constantly my source of frustration and self-deprecation. That night, I came out of my chrysalis of *rest* with new revelations about who I was and who I should be, and I found myself completely changed for the better.

I also felt the Lord tell me that night that it was time for "a new type of ministry." We had been struggling to get pregnant with our third child and a looming sense of doom seemed to overshadow Scriptures as I read them. I felt the Lord take me from one verse to another all across the Bible.

He told me things like, *Read up to here – now stop. This is what the verse means for you. Now go to this other passage,* and so forth. I began to cry as I sensed fear and anxiety forming in the pit of my stomach and up into my chest.

"A new type of ministry" was what God had told Dad right before he got sick. When those thoughts began to choke me, I asked God to please keep my family safe. I was willing to have anything done to me, but José and the kids – including future ones – needed to be safe. I begged Him not to let history repeat itself; I had already gone through too much. I didn't even want to be the one to get sick as I had as a child, because I knew what my kids would go through.

I prayed, *Yes, Lord. If you must, take me; but it's an awful thing to make happen all over again.*

I felt the warm comfort of Holy Spirit pour over me as God reassured me. I felt like He nearly *promised* me that nothing as damaging as what had happened to Dad would ever happen to us. I felt Him clarify that it didn't mean *nothing* would happen to us – we'd still get sick and have our share of struggles – but we wouldn't have to relive the type of illness my dad had.

Assured of that, I shared the word with José the next day. Within a few months, we sold our house for a profit, José quit his job to dedicate a full year to the ministry – whatever that looked like – and we learned that our third baby was healthy.

In 2003, after a year of ministering without an official job or paycheck, José was asked to become the executive pastor at our church. In addition, his previous job asked him to come back to a higher position, with a pay increase and bonuses! I was excited José was in ministry, using his gifts to serve and honor God at church and in his secular job. We were soaring.

In 2004, I began to feel anxious that I was not "in ministry" and felt stuck, as if I wasn't doing anything. A quick trip in and out of *this* chrysalis showed me that, through this season of growing and learning about myself, I was the minister of the most important group of people ever: my family. I poured myself into homeschooling and being the best wife and mommy I could be.

We had playgroups with other homeschoolers, we traveled with José's work across a few states, and we homeschooled in the mountains, desert, beaches, and the valley. We discovered discounts for homeschoolers all around Southern California, perfected our Thanksgiving meals, and enjoyed movie and pizza slumber parties after church on Sundays. I found myself so very happy and content with just *living* life.

Later that year, I hosted a table for our women's ministry Christmas event and felt drawn to do more with the women at our church. In 2005, God led me to approach the women's ministry director and let her know I would be available to help out in any way she saw fit. She asked me to speak at a women's retreat, and I loved it! I was so excited to start expanding my wings, and I wanted to soar.

I'll admit, those butterflies from my LABI speech class came back and I was a *mess* leading up to the moment I took the stand. But, once I did, Holy Spirit took over and it was powerful. That Christmas, I was prepared to host a table again and found out the event was canceled. I was bummed, and then the feeling of not doing *something* started creeping up again.

I was truly happy in the season I was in, I had entrusted my future to God, and I felt a release. I didn't understand why the uneasiness was coming back. The Lord showed me a Christmas tree with presents underneath. He helped me see that there was a gift meant for me – my time of ministry – but it wasn't to be opened until it was time. I could be assured it was mine and I *would* open it someday, but it was not yet time.

I sent an email to my pastor's wife explaining what I felt and asked her for prayer. She asked if she could give me a call later that week. As we spoke, I felt myself being released from the chrysalis yet again. The women's ministry director had resigned, and she offered *me* the position. I was excited and had so many ideas and plans. I was only thirty years old at the time and pregnant with my fourth baby. There were a few older ladies at church who initially felt I was too young, but God was faithful and I later received their full support. I found in them the prayer warriors that I still love to this day.

Approximately two hundred and fifty ladies were under my ministry, and I loved where I was. I took my kids with me everywhere. To this day, they're quite the ministry force to be reckoned with. I loved every aspect of women's ministry. I didn't mind staying up all night crafting something, sending out emails, or reminding the ladies I was praying for them. Our Mother's Day banquets became the main event of the year, and our Bible studies successfully ministered across the span of seven different cities in our valley. I had found my groove with homeschooling and leading the ladies. Ministering alongside me were the dream leadership board and amazing ladies in our church who came up to support us. I was soaring, and I had beautiful, capable, gifted, and inspiring people with me!

The year 2007 was rough. Not only had my dad passed away suddenly, but I faced additional physical and emotional challenges. My ministry mentor moved to a different state. I fell while exercising, busted my chin wide open, broke my front tooth above the gum-line, and went through multiple surgeries, bone grafts, and dental implants. All of this occurred within seven months. The financial debts for my fall were ridiculous.

As I crawled my way back into the chrysalis, riddled with agony in my heart, helplessness in my soul, chaos in my mind, and pain all over my body, I was defeated. I had lost my identity as "Peter's daughter," and my hope of an amazing ending to our story was gone. The one mentor I felt could help me walk through this spiritually had moved to another state, and I had literally lost a physical piece of me.

As the remaining pieces of my life lay fractured around me, I couldn't do anything but sit on the sofa with my four babies, watching their favorite shows and living life absorbed only by my kids and José.

Nothing else mattered. Not my ministry. Not my health. Not homeschooling. Nothing.

> *"Hide me in the shadow of Your wings."*
> Psalms 17:8b

While I numbly sat there, watching the world go on, God was working. And shaping. And recreating. And healing. Setting the trajectory of my life in a different direction than what I had dreamed, planned, desired, and hoped.

I believe I lasted in this season the longest. Perhaps it was a long season and I took my time coming out. But I eventually emerged – quite unsure of what I now looked like. I didn't know if I even liked myself, yet I was very much aware that things were brighter on the outside.

My husband and those around me were my lifesavers. They stood patiently outside the chrysalis while I was in there and made sure nothing from the outside disturbed the process nor the journey, and they were right there with me when it was time to fly!

As I mentioned, Christmas of 2008 was pivotal in my life. I unfolded my wings and watched as remnants of the colors I had newly absorbed took their form. Beautiful colors I had thought were part of me and hoped to keep were no longer necessary. The ones I needed were permanently part of me. The pulsing of a heart that once beat weakly on its own now beat stronger because of its awareness of *Who* was allowing it to beat. With each divinely appointed beat, my wings were made stronger and stronger.

In 2010, ministry at home started looking a little different. The charter school my kids attended allowed me to have a few days of free time, and I felt a growing desire to minister more deeply to our ladies. I no longer wanted to plan events where the ladies were ministered to by someone else; *I* personally wanted to be the one ministering to them.

At a board meeting dinner, I sat, frustrated, as we decided if lemon or chocolate cake went better with the Italian dinner at our women's retreat. I wanted to cry so bad at the longing in my heart that I pinched my thigh to get a grip on my emotions. I couldn't care less what the ladies were going to be consuming physically; I knew my role in the body of Christ was changing and I would be happy to see a more gifted planner handle those event details while I focused on what we would feed the women spiritually.

I struggled through our meeting. When I came home, I told José, "I want to focus on ministering to our ladies, not just *plan* things. I've loved everything we've been doing up until this point, but *now* I feel God isn't calling me to be an 'event planner.' I feel He's leading me to see lives *changed* through sharing His Word."

One Wednesday night after service, I was praying for one of our ladies who had recently lost her husband and was struggling with choices she needed to make regarding their daughter. We talked and prayed until everyone else left except for our pastor and José. When we finally came out of the room, my pastor looked at me and said he had already spoken with José. They both agreed it was time: I needed to get my minister's credentials.

For my thirty-fifth birthday, I gave myself the gift of completing the process to receive my minister's license. It wasn't easy. A few people didn't think it was appropriate for me, a woman, to get my license. But all that mattered to me was that God and the two men who were my spiritual covering believed in me. Later that year, I performed my first baptism as well as preached at a few other churches.

In 2012, for the very first time, Mom and I spoke together at our first women's event. The theme was "Once Upon a Time," and it centered on those moments where our dreams don't always come true, but God – the Author and Finisher of our faith – always assures us of a happy ending.

Mom and I wove our two testimonies of God's faithfulness throughout those thirty-two years Dad was alive, sharing her perspective as a wife and mother and my view as their daughter. We took turns conveying each pivotal moment of our lives, flying within each other's story, fluttering from one victory to the next. We shared times of learning and growth, those hard times of difficulty and change, and the wonder of soaring above it all as the Lord saw fit.

The pivotal moment of almost every character in the Bible involved laying down their own will, desires, and dreams to follow God's perfect plan for their lives. While we can read their stories from beginning to end, their journey must have been difficult, and their destination must have surpassed their wildest dreams. People can tell you how to live a life of complete surrender, but it's a rare gift to watch God's Word come to life with someone you love and respect as I have with my mom. Sharing the platform with my mom was such a defining time in my life and a memory I will cherish forever.

Using that message, I began to note more detailed information about each season I had spoken about. I kept simple notes of each chapter of my life, some of which I shared when I preached, while others I kept for myself. People would tell me, "You should write a book," and I would smile as I jotted down more notes as they came to me.

Later that year, not only was I able to organize a powerful women's conference, but I also brought various speakers together and shared the platform. I was ministering to my family, the ladies at my church, and, on occasion, other groups outside our church.

At a district women's conference we attended, a chrysalis was the center focal point of the stage. On the first day of the conference, we wrote down our prayer requests, dreams, and struggles. During prayer time, we were instructed to go and place our papers inside a hole at the top of the chrysalis.

The next morning, to our surprise, there was a butterfly in its place with what looked like tissue paper all over its wings. As the event progressed, we came to realize that the things we had written down were now what decorated the wings of the butterfly. I was blown away.

We incorporated the message of the chrysalis into our very own retreat, a message that would impact my life *very* powerfully.

José, the kids, and I were living and serving faithfully at church. By this time, José was on the teaching team and our kids were involved with church programs. They all used their talents to help at our women's events.

And then it started *again*. That feeling.

I sat in our women's board meeting and told my team, "I can't quite place it, but I sense God's placing me in a *chrysalis*."

As I informed the ladies I was being placed in a chrysalis, I still had no idea what that meant.

Happy and satisfied with where we were serving in ministry, I told José that maybe we had heard wrong. When we were young and felt called to the ministry, maybe we thought we were supposed to be *lead* pastors of a church, but perhaps we have *hearts* of pastors where we can come alongside our pastors, care as much as they do for their sheep, and help them accomplish the things God has placed on *their* hearts.

"Maybe we're just that faithful family that pastors can trust to come alongside them in ministry," I told José.

He didn't seem to agree. Since Bible college, José had always been bi-vocational, meaning he held a full-time job working outside the church and ministered at church simultaneously. His heart beat for the day he could commit himself to ministry without depending on a secular job.

Our church adopted another church in Bishop, California, and José was asked to be on the preaching team. We drove six hours up on Fridays after he got out of work, spent Saturdays exploring the town, ministered on Sundays, and returned on Sunday evenings. We were asked to consider taking the church full-time. After much prayer, discussion, and an interesting "sign" from the Lord, we knew we weren't meant to permanently stay. We continued making trips on the weekends.

In the middle of the night in May of 2013, I had a dream that I was dying. I was putting all our affairs in order and I told my cousin Marina where everything was so my family wouldn't struggle. In my dream, I told her, "Please make sure to tell my kids *every day* that I love them. That they were everything I had ever wanted and my gifts from God." And then I said, "I only wish I could have done more."

This was strange because I had grown up with friends who were ministry kids who left the ministry or struggled in life because their parents had chosen ministry over them. My mom would have me stay with my Nana while she ministered to the youth or during choir practices, and I hated being left behind. I determined my kids would do ministry *with* me and go with me as much as possible to every event I attended.

I also made sure we had tons of fun the week before an event. Then, the week of the event the kids knew to let Mommy focus and be helpful around the house and with each other. The very evening the event was over, I would bring back treats for the kids and we would recuperate together by watching movies and having fun. I always made sure to sandwich a week of ministry focus with lots of fun attention for the kids.

Wishing I could have "done more" in my dream made no sense. I didn't have any regrets, so why would I say that? I awoke and picked up my Bible. The Lord led me to Isaiah 60. As I read, I came to realize that my "death" from the dream was God's sign that I needed to step down from women's ministry. Interestingly, the chapter in Isaiah included sons and daughters returning home as well as other countries helping to build up God's temple once again.

Not long after I had that dream, another church asked our Temecula church to adopt them as well. This time, the church was in Long Beach,

California. The same preaching team was asked to take turns. They also asked José to oversee the team and its preaching rotation. José and the kids went down to see the church. He came back excited about how beautiful it was and that he felt inspired to ask our pastor if we could take the church completely.

We became the campus pastors of CrossRoads Church, Long Beach on September 8, 2013. Commuting from Menifee meant a long trip down the 91 freeway every Sunday and occasionally during the week. We woke up at 5:00 a.m. to make it to Long Beach with enough time to set everything up, get dressed, and minister at each Sunday service.

During our time there, we not only renovated the 1950s building, but we also established an entire worship team, children's ministry, youth ministry, and several outreaches. We had awesome co-pastors in Paul and Lala Montano, our ministry partners from Temecula, and we built up an amazing ministry team, which included our own kids.

When I had served as the children's pastor in Fallbrook in the mid-1990s, our Spanish congregation held services in a small side building of the larger church. I used to work cleaning the main sanctuary and classrooms. The church itself was pretty spotless, and there wasn't much to do. At nineteen years old, I wondered if anyone would *really* notice if I didn't clean every corner of the bathroom. I heard the Lord say, *En lo poco se fiel, sobre mucho te pondré.* Be faithful with the little and I'll place you in charge of more. I learned to do my work right because God Himself was my boss overseeing my work.

Another time, I was in the sanctuary and I heard it again: *Be faithful with the little and I'll place you in charge of more.* I looked around at the beautiful high ceilings, the rows and rows of church pews, and the stained glass. By looking at the size of it all, I never could imagine what God meant. I had never been in such a beautiful building, let alone thought of having one of my own.

But in 2013, as I found myself in Long Beach wiping years of grime off the backs of benches and staring down rows and rows of church pews I still had left to clean, I thought to myself, *Is this worth it? Will anybody really notice?*

Then the Lord opened my eyes. After eighteen years of faithfully working in God's house – cleaning bathrooms, caring for children and youth, singing on the worship team, ministering to ladies, driving hours to serve, and doing all things as unto the Lord who saw everything – I was now caring for the *more* He had promised me. I cried as I diligently cleaned those pews, the ones God Himself had faithfully given us.

Chapter Fifteen

EMERGING

"Blessed be the God and Father of our Lord Jesus Christ, the Father of mercies and God of all comfort, who comforts us in all our affliction, so that we may be able to comfort those who are in any affliction, with the comfort with which we ourselves are comforted by God."
2 Corinthians 1:3-4

Amazing things occur in the darkness of the chrysalis. Unless a caterpillar enters the chrysalis, it will never become a butterfly. The chrysalis is necessary. Though just for a season, it proves to be the most important season for that caterpillar.

To the eye watching from the outside, nothing is happening. Everything is still. Quiet. Lonely. Boring.

But oh, the processes that are happening on the inside! Majestic ones. Unfathomable changes that can never be appreciated in advance, but only after emerging from the darkness and solitude of the chrysalis. No one can appreciate the process more than the one who has lived it.

It is then that we discover the beauty of who we've become, and we learn how we are meant to share ourselves and experiences with others. When we allow the process to serve its purpose, we can help others see God in their own situations.

I want to go back and tell my younger self how amazing these moments can be if we trust the One who weaves around us the very things that help us transform into the creation He desires us to be. I'm sure she would have walked with her head up more often. She may have avoided creating defense mechanisms and instead opened herself up more to the world around her. She may have trusted people more or faced conflict head-on, knowing God would defend her without worrying about pleasing others or what they thought about her. Instead of feeling like she always had to be in control because the world around her seemed so chaotic at times, I think I could have helped her not feel like she had anything to prove or enshroud herself in doing things perfectly.

"As for God, His way is perfect; The word of the Lord is proven;
He is a shield to all who trust in Him."
Psalms 18:30 (KJV)

Each season of increasing growth, intense struggle, and divine victory in my life resembled the same life cycle of a caterpillar to a chrysalis to a butterfly. With every season when I couldn't get enough of God's Word, worship, and learning, I was preparing for something new. The hungrier I was, the faster I was going to grow and change. Slower seasons meant slower growth. Those moments of tests and trials resembled chrysalis moments, and I learned the sooner I allowed the change to mold and shape me, the better. When things in life were soaring, I knew it was the splendor of God seeing me fit to accomplish the things set out before me.

Did you know that after a butterfly emerges from the chrysalis, there's a *pause*? The butterfly must pause to let its entire body that's filled up with liquid to fill its wings and dry. Before the pause there's a *struggle*. No one but the butterfly can struggle to emerge from the chrysalis or else great damage can occur to the butterfly, making flying impossible.

Before the struggle is the call to *emerge* forth from out of the chrysalis.

The night of my strange dream about dying was not just the beginning of our journey toward becoming lead pastors. That night, God made it clear I was to pull out my notes I had written throughout my life – a small egg of a book – and finish writing it. I was told to *emerge* and sit down with a focus on writing my book. *This* book. So, I hungrily fought to get it finished, remembering and learning all I could about God's hand throughout my journey.

It was a struggle to get every important thing about my life down on paper. I cried as past pains resurfaced, and I winced at mistakes I wished I had never made. And, as I worked on this book, the Lord worked on my heart. As I wrote each story, I reflected on God's *providential hand* over my life, His *sovereignty* over my path, His *mercy* over my soul, His *grace* over my mistakes, and His *heartbeat* over mine . . . And I cried some more.

I finished the manuscript, expecting to print it right away, but the Lord gave me peace that He would send someone to help me publish it. So, the book was put on *pause* and I was able to focus on our church in Long Beach.

The church grew amazingly and our hearts started venturing more and more toward making Long Beach our permanent home. Sometimes we spent the night at church over the weekend or got a hotel so we could be near as we worked on special events. It was hard to build relationships with our growing church family when we lived so far away.

We figured the amount we were spending on hotels could be used to pay for a small studio apartment. The six of us were technically living in a hotel room over the weekends. If we could survive that, then why not our own place, however small?

We started our search and found the perfect place, something we could work with in the nice part of Long Beach's art district. We prayed and approached our home church with the prospect of moving. We were given the okay with some parameters. But in the few months we spent trying to figure things out, that rental unit had nearly doubled in price!

We had fallen in love with the people of Long Beach, and we watched with sheer sadness as the prospect of being full-time lead pastors slipped from our grasp. Much to our dismay, it was becoming obvious that it wasn't God's will.

In February of 2017, we said goodbye. Our heart's calling was to be lead pastors of our own church. Months before, the Lord had given José the outline of what our church was going to be like. The Lord had even given José the name we would call our church. We thought it would happen in the near future if we continued on the path we were on.

Later that year, I was given a last-minute invitation to the conference of a Christian best-selling author my friend had won tickets to. We'd had the same author speak at one of our very *own* conferences when I was the women's ministry director, and I felt compelled to accept the invitation. I was still healing from having to leave our Long Beach church, so I waited to the side while my friend had the author sign a copy of her book. All of a sudden, my friend turned around and gestured for me to come over. I reluctantly went over and was introduced to her.

"Hello," I said. "We've met before. You spoke at our women's event in Temecula."

She talked about her time at our church, recalling facts about our event that proved she wasn't just trying to be polite.

And *then,* with little control of my own volition, I heard myself say, "My family has been keeping you in prayer, and if you ever need anything at all, please let me know. I speak Spanish, can read and write decently, and whatever I can't do, I'm sure I can find someone."

To my surprise, she handed me her card with her personal phone number, asked me to call her, and within weeks I found myself serving on her ministry team. God has allowed our friendship to grow. She has proven to be a mentor in every aspect of my life and ministry that I cherish dearly.

That same year, we sold our Menifee home and settled our finances so we could be in the best position possible for wherever God would lead us next. We were intentional to visit as many churches as we could, learning what they did right and taking notes for what we would want to incorporate into our next church. We asked God to close all the wrong doors - open doors are easy to walk through - and we watched as He closed door after door.

We found a few prospects in churches that were already established, but the doors we pursued were soundly shut by the Lord. We hesitantly had conversations about church planting – something we had been asked to do during our years in Long Beach. José was offered lucrative jobs in other states, but when we tried to walk through those doors in obedience, they were all shut as well.

We realized that back in 2016, the Lord had made José pull over on the freeway, under the overpass of *Nuevo Road*, which means "new road." The Lord was preparing our family for a *new* path.

We knew our next church would be in the same area where we lived so we could build relationships with our community. This made a huge difference in making our decisions.

"And after you have suffered a little while, the God of all grace, who has called you to His eternal glory in Christ, **will Himself restore, confirm, strengthen, and establish you.***"*
1 Peter 5:10, emphasis mine

In 2018, we found ourselves back in Temecula, California. After much prayer, some tears, advice, wise counsel, and permission, we boarded an airplane to Ohio for church planting training. Upon our return, we arrived with a notebook filled with our strategic plan. We spent the year praying, fasting, writing, editing, and planning. Finally, on January 26, 2019, we held our first prayer meeting and announced we would launch CityWide Mosaic, Temecula.

Apparently, we angered the enemy as a ripple of distractions and attacks headed toward us, turning into a tsunami that hit our family with one wave after another. We pushed forward with what we were called to do. Although the Lord did not remove the attacks, He mercifully gave us the words "be still" each time.

We braced for impact sheltered in the embrace of His chrysalis, aware that He shielded us from the brunt of these hits. We were molded and shaped as warriors.

In the middle of the battle, I felt the most defeated I had ever been since deciding to plant a church; yet, I refused to let that keep me knocked down. I became aware that everything I had learned about needing to wear the armor of God was a reality more than ever before.

At the lowest point of that season, God blew me away and surprised me. I was asked to speak at a camp. While it was currently called Girls Ministries Camp, many years before I had known it as *Missionette Camp*!

I would be speaking at the very same camp that had radically changed the trajectory of my life. The same camp where I had the most powerful encounters with God, where I received my calling into the ministry – *this* current ministry. What an honor!

The theme that year was "Princess Warrior of God." As I stood on the platform, I shared the very message God had called me to share back when I was exactly where those girls sat: *Your Dad.* The Creator of the universe loved them so much that Jesus came to die for their sins so they could also have victory in their battles as princess warriors through the power and anointing of Holy Spirit. As He was with me, God was *their* Abba Father and He alone would be with them to help them conquer all things!

> *"When the enemy comes in like a flood, The Spirit of*
> *the LORD will lift up a standard against him."*
> Isaiah 59:19 (KJV)

We officially opened our church doors as CityWide Mosaic inside a country line dancing bar on January 12, 2020. God was saving lives, our ministry team was growing, our church was advancing against enemy territory, there were healings and prophetic words spoken over us and through us, and we watched as children came back home to their families *and* the Lord. We also watched as some of our own children from when we had been children's pastors in Fallbrook – now adults themselves with families of their own – came and ministered alongside us in their own gifting and calling right here at CityWide Mosaic.

Then March of 2020 hit.

Our folder with our strategic plan went out the door as we, along with the rest of the world, reconfigured what life was supposed to look like. God's grace carried us through as we forged ahead, very much aware that God was in control, leading us beyond what we could have imagined.

And He *still* is.

God never promises us that life will be *perfect* if we are His children. He never promises we won't have any struggles or heartaches. He doesn't promise that ninety percent of our lives will be happy and right and only ten percent of it will be difficult.

> *"He makes his sun rise on the evil and on the good,*
> *and sends rain on the just and on the unjust."*
> Matthew 5:45

God promises that no matter what happens in life, good or bad, right or wrong, we will be *held*. He will hold us in the very palm of His hands.

> *"Behold, I have engraved you on the palms of My hands;*
> *your walls are continually before Me."*
> Isaiah 49:16

Throughout the *stages* of my life, I've had low moments of crawling and barely making it as well as seasons where I was so hungry for God and grew so much. Then there were seasons when He would place me in His chrysalis to emerge into someone new, someone more in His likeness, His *Imago Dei*, only to have the whole process repeat all over again and again and *again*. I haven't mastered it yet, but I do find it easier to recognize each stage in my own life and the lives of others.

Life can be hard. Most of you reading this already know that. We don't always get what we want. Life hurts us, and we hurt others sometimes. No matter what happens in life, God loves us. I want you to understand that a life with God is the best life ever because He alone helps us survive the various seasons we will go through.

My desire for writing this book is to encourage you to see God's love for you in *each* season. He is sovereign and omniscient, and, because of that, you can trust Him. Each stage carries highs and lows. The risks, responsibilities, and rewards all occur to take us from glory to glory, shaping us more and more into His likeness and *Imago Dei*. To encounter God in each season is to experience the greatest spiritual metamorphosis one could ever imagine. Throughout the journey, we have the privilege, responsibility, and honor to reveal God to those around us.

> *"All this is from God, who through Christ reconciled us to Himself and **gave us the ministry of reconciliation**; that is, in Christ, God was reconciling the world to Himself, not counting their trespasses against them, and **entrusting to us the message of reconciliation**. Therefore, we are ambassadors for Christ, God making His appeal through us. We implore you on behalf of Christ, be reconciled to God. For our sake He made Him to be sin who knew no sin, so that in Him we might become the righteousness of God."*
> 2 Corinthians 5:18-21, emphasis mine

Most importantly, if you don't already have a relationship with our gracious and loving God who transforms us in His chrysalis, I want to make sure you understand that God sent His son Jesus Christ to die for your sins. If you've ever lied, looked at someone in an inappropriate way, let your anger get the best of you, or withheld love from someone . . . you've sinned.

We deserve to be punished for our sins; we deserve to die because of our sins. But God – in His mercy and love – came in human form and died for our sins so that we wouldn't have to. That is *so* much more than we ever deserve.

Simply admit that you've sinned and put your faith in Jesus as God to be made in right standing with Him. He will welcome you into a relationship with Him. He is your Abba Father who cares for you and loves you. There is no better place to be than in God's presence, allowing

Him to fill every part of your life. Let Him cover those things that spin around in your head, that cause your heart to beat at a faster pace, that cause your soul to cry out. You'll find that in His presence there is fullness of joy and that His love surrounds and fills you, completely.

May you grow in awareness that, regardless of the season you are in, you are in *His chrysalis*, and He is carefully and lovingly weaving you more and more into His image. There is no better place to be!

AFTERWORD

As I complete this book, I can't help but think of the journey I've been on. I wrote different chapters at various seasons of my life, and the book truly started taking shape in 2012 when I felt the sense of urgency from the Lord to finish. Ten years later, I'm in my mid-forties and find myself teetering between my life that *was* and the one I'm *approaching*. If I'm transparent, I'm nervous about what tomorrow brings, but confident in the One who writes my story.

It's 2022 at the time of editing. José and I celebrated our twenty-fifth anniversary in May. Mom married Reverend Alex Najar and she is now enjoying traveling the world. She continues to minister at church and is regularly asked to speak.

My youngest son Joseph is days away from starting his senior year of high school and praying about where he will attend college. His future plans include reaching youth for Christ, owning his own business, and traveling the world.

Joscelyn is currently working on her minister's credentials to become a children's pastor and has proven to be quite an asset on so many levels at CityWide Mosaic.

Karissa is working at an art studio, planning her next trip, and starting a new adventure as a Youth Ministries Leader at CityWide Mosaic.

Designs and artwork for this book and upcoming publications are hers. Karissa was mindful that each piece has its own symbolism from throughout my life.

Caitlyn has married Salvador David Santillan and both are faithfully serving the Lord at their home church. They have their own photography business, and we are expecting our *first* grandbaby in January of 2023! The day we found out about Caitlyn's baby, Mom and I stood crying in her hallway in a tight embrace. We remembered when it was just the two of us facing a future unknown and were in sheer adoration and gratitude for God's faithfulness yet again.

I've asked to be called Nana, a name I hold in the highest esteem with full understanding of the privilege this role holds. I picked up her baton when my Nana went home to be with Jesus.

This story is a legacy entrusted to me, and now I pass it on to the next generations. I stand in the middle, looking back at my father, mother, and grandparents and looking forward to my children and their children's children. It's a surreal honor to conclude writing this book, passing along my own personal knowledge of who God is to me, to those yet to come. I'm beyond excited to feed God's Word into those precious lives, encourage them in their own times inside His chrysalis, and watch them soar as Abba Father lifts them up so they, too, can *fly*!

FROM NOW UNTO THOSE THAT COME . . .

"Only be careful, and watch yourselves closely **so that you do not forget** *the things your eyes have seen or let them slip from your heart as long as you live. Teach them to your children and to their children after them."*
Deuteronomy 4:9 (NIV, emphasis mine)

www.judyperezvelazquez.com

India Ebook's

Questions Bank

FOR IGNOU MPS-001

POLITICAL THEORY

MA-POLITICAL SCIENCE

MPS - FIRST YEAR

JANMEJOY DAS

INDIA EBOOK PRESS